The Wisdom
of
Master Nuno Oliveira

by Antoine de Coux

Introduction by

Suzanne Laurenty

Translated to English

By Jean Philippe Giacomini

XENOPHON PRESS

Original edition:
Paroles du Maître Nuno Oliveira, by Antoine de Coux,
© Editions Belin - Paris 2007,
ISBN 9782701145860

Title: *The Wisdom of Master Nuno Oliveira,* by Antoine de Coux
Copyright © 2012 by Xenophon Press LLC

Translated by Jean Philippe Giacomini

Edited by Richard F. Williams and Frances A. Williams

Cover design by Naia Poyer

Published by Xenophon Press LLC

7518 Bayside Road,

Franktown, Virginia 23354-2106, U.S.A.

XenophonPress@gmail.com

ISBN-10   0933316305
ISBN-13   9780933316300

2

The Wisdom
of
Master Nuno Oliveira

By Antoine de Coux

Introduction by

Suzanne Laurenty

Translated to English

By Jean Philippe Giacomini

Edited by Richard and Frances Williams

XENOPHON PRESS LIBRARY

30 Years with Master Nuno Oliveira, Michel Henriquet 2011
A Rider's Survival From Tyranny, Charles de Kunffy 2012
Another Horsemanship, Jean-Claude Racinet, 1994
Art of the Lusitano, Pedro Yglesias de Oliveira 2012
Baucher and His School, General Decarpentry 2011
Dressage in the French Tradition, Dom Diogo de Bragança 2011
École de Cavalerie Part II (School of Horsemanship),
        François Robichon de la Guérinière 1992
François Baucher: The Man and His Method, Hilda Nelson 2012
*From the Real Picaria of the 18th Century to the Portuguese School
        of Equestrian Art,* Yglesias de Oliveira and da Costa 2012
Healing Hands, Dominique Giniaux, DVM 1998
Methodical Dressage of the Riding Horse, and *Dressage of the
        Outdoor Horse*, Faverot de Kerbrech 2010
The Spanish Riding School in Vienna and *Piaffe and Passage,*
        General Decarpentry 2012
Racinet Explains Baucher, Jean-Claude Racinet 1997
The Écuyères of the 19th Century in the Circus, Hilda Nelson 2001
The Gymnasium of the Horse, Gustav Steinbrecht 2011
The Handbook of Jumping Essentials, François Lemaire de Ruffieu
        1997
The Legacy of Master Nuno Oliveira, Stephanie Millham 2013
The Maneige Royal, Antoine de Pluvinel 2010
Total Horsemanship, Jean-Claude Racinet 1999
What the Horses have Told me, Dominique Giniaux, DVM 1996

Available at **www.XenophonPress.com**

TABLE OF CONTENTS

PUBLISHER'S INTRODUCTION

Antoine de Coux, Secretary of State to Master Nuno Oliveira

It is with great joy that we bring this translation to light. Antoine de Coux took notes in multiple courses and lessons with Nuno Oliveira. He carefully documented not only his own, but the lessons of many others. Enclosed here is advice for a wide variety of riders and horses. His journals contain the Master's principles which include necessary repetition of important concepts, reiterated, and rephrased with subtle changes. We feel this was a key technique that the Master used to underline, through repetition, the most important information. The fact that the Master repeats these ideas suggests the need of the rider and here, the reader to hear them again. Antoine de Coux has given us the privilege of auditing Master Nuno Oliveira's teaching anew.

Sadly, Antoine de Coux did not live to see the work completed. His dedicated colleagues finished the project and brought it to French readers. Antoine de Coux jokingly called himself "Secretary of State to Master Nuno Oliveira." We are eternally grateful for this stewardship of information.

Finding a willing translator who speaks the language, knows the subject, and the characters is a very difficult task. We are especially grateful to have J.P. Giacomini's accurate translation of the wisdom of the Master he knew well. English readers have J.P. to thank for this translation. Added in square brackets [ ] are all of J.P.'s notes. These fall into four types: cases where we have re-stated the word from the French text, notes that help clarify the flow and understanding of the text to the English reader, footnotes with added information cross-referencing concepts presented elsewhere in the book, and footnotes detailing J.P.'s personal knowledge of the techniques of Nuno Oliveira, and historical references.

Nuno Oliveira was a giant in the history of horsemanship. Certainly in the 20th Century, he embodied the synthesis of the best of horsemanship passed down to us. Far from being nationalistic, Oliveira was pragmatic, practical--he used the methods that worked with most riders, with most horses, most of the time. His theories were tested by daily practice on countless horses. By this definition, his horsemanship was truly classical.

We are grateful to all of Nuno Oliveira's students who keep his art alive. Through efforts of note-taking, teaching, riding, training, and authorship the legacy and *Wisdom of Master Nuno Oliveira* continues to benefit horses and riders today.

-Richard and Frances Williams, Xenophon Press LLC

TRANSLATOR'S PREFACE

Nuno Oliveira, the greatest
equestrian intelligence of the 20th century

At sixteen, I started my quest for a higher form of horsemanship. Simply said, I was trying to get a clue on the how-and-why of what I had been doing on horseback "by the seat of my pants." I had ridden lots of colts, done a bit of eventing, show-jumping and rode (without great success) in steeple-chase races. My new passion was dressage and I had trained a few horses to do my bidding, in some approximate way. Prompted by the encouragements of my mentor Georges Caubet, who was one of the early French visitors to the school of the Portuguese classical Master Nuno Oliveira, and after a day spent watching Michel Henriquet ride his wonderfully trained horses, I realized that there was more to riding than I had experienced thus far. As a result, I visited Portugal for the first time to study for one month with Oliveira during the holidays. The day I arrived at his school, the Master casually asked me if I knew how to do a "shoulder-in" and I assured him that I did. "Can you do a 'half-pass'?" I got a little suspicious of where this conversation was leading. With already less assurance, I told him that: "Yes, I have done some." "How about a circle?" In a little voice, I uttered: "I think I can," preparing myself for some form of rebuke. Instead came his tongue-in-cheek, yet sincere, answer: "You are one lucky rider: I have been attempting to ride a perfect circle for 40 years and I hope I will soon succeed." In this ironic statement lays the entire secret of horsemanship: rather than exclusively pursuing the pride of showing-off one's talent by performing difficult tricks (or higher levels of competition), a dedicated rider must always work at perfecting the simplest exercises.

This was my introduction to the mind of the man who became my teacher and the inspiration of my professional life. Forty six years later, the translation of this important book brings back to my memory the sentences I heard over and over in the tiny indoor manege of the Quinta da Chafariz in Povoa de Santo Adriao, a few miles from Lisbon. During that first visit, I met Antoine de Coux who was also on his first voyage to the place he would return to for many years. We became fast friends and I later visited Antoine in Belgium. He had a wise attitude acquired through many years on the judicial bench and an inquiring mind passionate about his discovery of dressage. I returned for a year in 1970, which I spent riding Oliveira's wonderful schoolmasters. More importantly, I had the opportunity to start five young stallions under Oliveira's daily supervision.

7

This experience instilled in me the fundamental importance of impulsion through forward movement as the basis for all training. Later on, I took a job as assistant trainer at the national stud of Alter do Chão (where the Alter Real horses of the Portuguese School of Equestrian Art are bred). For nearly four years at the National stud, I was the student of Dom Jose Athayde, head rider of the stud and himself a very distinguished disciple of Master Oliveira. In Alter, I rode all the stallions previously trained by Athayde and Dr. Borba, as well as many more colts, following Oliveira's approach.

I lost contact with Antoine and it is not without emotion that I read the amazing work of compilation of all those notes he had taken tirelessly during two and a half decades of loyal and attentive study. They contain many repetitions that are used to underline the preoccupation of Oliveira with some fundamental concepts he held dear. It was Antoine's hope that this system would really etch these ideas in the mind of the readers who had not benefitted from Oliveira's direct teaching. To help the reader better understand the context of each advice that is not self-explanatory, I have taken the liberty to insert notes in brackets [   ] to clarify the ideas expressed, all based on my own observations of his training. It is my hope that the English-speaking readers will find these added notes helpful to their understanding of the work. To paraphrase Norman Maclean's *A River Runs Through It,* we could say of Nuno Oliveira: "To him, all good things--dressage as well as eternal salvation--come by grace and grace comes by art and art does not come easy." This book is about making the art of training horses a little bit easier for the many admirers of Master Nuno Oliveira eager to know his secrets.

Nuno Oliveira was a spiritual man deeply interested in the human condition and in his art, dressage, as a vehicle for the elevation of the soul. If his teaching was inspired by his artistic aspirations and got him lost into philosophical musings from time to time, he never forgot that for him as well as for his students, "art doesn't come easy." His teaching was always very practical: a few basic principles we must always remember and a thousand details that take a long time to observe, understand and resolve. He had learned his craft through a very long and intense practice of training literally hundreds of horses into all the difficulties of Equestrian Art, but also by reading all the French books he found in the library of one of his early patrons, Manuel de Barros. Oliveira's work was a perfect synthesis of intelligent and selective erudition with immense experience. It is our luck to be able to benefit from the results of this rare combination.

In his clinics and his daily lessons at his farm, most of the students were under the spell of his mystique and they adored deciphering the sometimes cryptic advice and the entertaining stories. But the ones who really succeeded later as horse trainers paid attention to the minutia of what Oliveira taught. A famous general said that "In love as in war, success resides in the execution." This is also completely true of horse training. Sometimes there are apparent contradictions in what the Master said, but that is because there are many practical exceptions to the rules according to the horse, to the moment and to the goal pursued. To quote again Norman Maclean's *A River Runs Through It*, which tells us a lot of interesting things about acquiring mastery: "That's one trouble with hanging around a Master--you pick up some of his stuff, like how to cast into a bush, but you use it just when the Master is doing the opposite." I hope the notes included in the text will explain as much as possible, some of the conditions in which Oliveira's teachings were applied.

Oliveira insisted that he was, above all, interested in results much more than in dressage theories, though he knew them all. His exceptional equestrian intelligence resided in the fact that he knew when to do what, and which author's advice was useful at which moment and which advice had no real value. Oliveira's art was greater than the sum of all the knowledge he assembled from the relevant authors who came before him. He had a unique perspective on dressage because he really "owned" all the information he had acquired through trying out the techniques he learned from the books. The Master told me once in a conversation, "I have tried everything in dressage." He meant every technique, every bit, every rein, until proven useful or useless. He had no taboos or dogmatic allegiance. Thanks to that immense curiosity he discovered the ideas that led to the simplification of his principles based either on La Guérinière, Steinbrecht or Baucher and the multiplication of his techniques adapted to the many training situations he encountered. All of his choices were not made in blind reverence to the past, but because they were supremely effective while always respecting the emotional, mental and physical well-being of the horse.

One of Oliveira's leading preoccupations was the lightness of the horse's response to the aids, which implies that the rider always tries to do less whenever possible, but never hesitates to do as much as warranted by occasional resistances. He relentlessly insisted that this lightness must be the result of a constant impulsion rather than the pernicious abandonment of the contact. His driving idea is the roundness of the horse: the slight lift of the back, the tilting of the pelvis, the soft arching of the neck. Another leading concept is the cadence that must be as slow as possible without losing an ounce of energy. Though you will find many mentions of putting weight on the hind-end of the horse in order to make sure the balance is not on the forehand, the equilibrium Oliveira preferred was quite horizontal with equal weight on both ends of the horse, as we can see in his pictures and movies. He did not elevate the poll very much like Baucher's Second Manner (an idea he abandoned after a period of exploration in his youth), nor did he lower the quarters as much as La Guérinière did. He preferred a conservative approach that did not force the horse and built the collection by the engagement of the hind legs under the body rather than reporting weight backward by the incessant use of half-halts as in the German system. In Oliveira's mind this is the true difference between true collection and compression. To him, training collection consists of applying "a million comprehensive effects (*effet d'ensemble* that relaxes the horse under the combined effect of the spurs and hand), followed by a million 'yielding of the aids' (*descente de main et de jambes*)." The result is a horse that stays in self-carriage as "on freedom on *parole*" and "enjoys himself in the airs and movements he is performing."

A peculiarity of Oliveira's work was the very slow, but very energetic walk he preferred to practice the gymnastic exercises that he used systematically to develop suppleness, balance and straightness. This slow walk was one of his signatures and the way he managed to create that much energy in the walk had a lot to do with his other great achievement: slow, calm and elevated piaffes. This book contains much practical advice on sequences of exercises designed to resolve particular problems, specifically the work of young horses. Great detail is given on the use of the shoulder-in that Oliveira called the "aspirin of equitation" because of its value in resolving so many problems. Of note is the use of his rational approach to counter-canter that is different from the accepted practice and permits a much earlier improvement of the balance at the canter. The Master had no qualms about using draw reins when necessary and explains their positive use in several applications. All of this work collected through twenty years of lessons observed by Antoine de Coux in real time is eminently useful and deserves to be read over and over until fully absorbed.

Oliveira's work may be called classical, but a better description would be classic[1] because it is a work for the ages that represents the culmination of four centuries of development of the Art. He achieved real equestrian wisdom through the selection he made for our benefit of all concepts developed before him. Oliveira's work cannot be hijacked by one faction or another as it is not based on any dogmatism or political correctness. It is "reality training" at its best and it is applicable to all

---

[1]   Of the first or highest quality, class, or rank; of or adhering to an established set of artistic or scientific standards or methods.

fields of horsemanship. After my years of study in Portugal, and a stay in Spain, I eventually ended up in England training international level dressage, eventing and show jumping horses and I never had to deviate from the training principles I learned under Oliveira and his disciple Dom Jose Athayde. In the hundreds of clinics I have given since I left Portugal in 1975, though I have added a few techniques of my own to resolve the many problems that appear with remedial horses I frequently encounter, I have always gone back to the teachings of Nuno Oliveira as the core of my approach. I am grateful to Xenophon Press for the opportunity of translating this major book because it made me the first beneficiary of its information by reminding me of all I forgot.

Oliveira is singly responsible for the emergence of Portugal as a beacon of good horsemanship in the 20th century. Through his disciples Dr. Guilherme Borba and Dr. Joao Filipe Graciosa, he has influenced the formation of both the Royal Spanish School of Equestrian Art and the Portuguese School of Equestrian Art. In turn, many of those riders have become successful competitors and teachers and are now influencing new generations of excellent riders. There is a fallacy today that classical dressage is different from competitive dressage. Michel Henriquet, the French disciple of the Master demonstrated this concept brilliantly by training his wife Catherine to become French dressage champion and an Olympic rider. My belief is the supposed difference between classical and competitive work is only true in the sense that some riders choose to ignore the concept of lightness and get away with it because judges are bound to grade what is in front of them, not the method by which the horses have been trained. Nuno Oliveira's teachings can be used to train any kind of horse for the FEI disciplines just as much as horses trained purely for art's sake.

Horsemanship is in constant change through the breeding of better and better horses, clinics by international experts, and access we are gaining to riders in all corners of the world through the internet. Somebody may well improve on Oliveira's contribution to horsemanship but it will only happen if the next innovator has first studied his work in-depth and practiced on a lot of horses in order to add to the existing knowledge, not delude themselves into re-inventing what has already existed for a century or two. There is no revolution in horsemanship, only evolution and Master Oliveira is the standard of today.

On a final note, I want to recall a conversation that stuck in my memory. It happened in 1970 when I was back in Portugal studying dressage full time. During the morning class, as Master Oliveira was growing impatient with the eight or ten of us struggling with the difficulties of self-control on a horse, he stopped us in our tracks. Adopting the dramatic stance that he used when delving away from *Haute-Ecole* into philosophical digression, he asked: "Why do you ride horses?" One by one, embarrassed by having to publicly reveal our unresolved equestrian secrets, we muffled some unsatisfactory answers. Eventually, the Master articulated his profession of faith: "I ride horses because I love them."

All of us remained silent, oscillating between embarrassment and cynicism. The great Master could not just have that reason alone to ride horses, did I think in the certainty of my twenty years of age. Well, he did! His riding demonstrated what he declared: he loved his horses and his horses loved him back. Riding was a romantic endeavor for Master Oliveira. His passion for his personal horses was only equalled by his fascination for the training process that he studied in depth, supremely practiced and improved significantly for the common benefit of horses and humans.

His passionate life may have sometimes reflected a very complex personality, but when he was on a horse (which was most of his waking hours), he was disciplined and selfless, yet completely involved in the artistic emotions that made his soul resonate. I believe he was happy in a profound way when he was on a horse. The more time went on, the more his conversation and his writings reflected a deep concern for the morality of horsemanship. His life, like the ones of many great artists, seemed a battlefield between the erring of the ego and his divinely inspired love for his equine partners with whom he practiced his chosen media, Equestrian Art. I think love definitely won.

-Jean Philippe Giacomini, translator and devoted disciple

THE WISDOM
OF
MASTER NUNO OLIVEIRA

INTRODUCTION

Nuno Oliveira, the great, maybe the greatest *écuyer*[2] of the last century had few negative critics. On the other hand, he has had numerous admirers. Better yet, he had loyal students and unconditional friends. Amongst them was Antoine de Coux.

Antoine de Coux, a magistrate in the Belgian Congo, on his way back to Belgium, stops one day in Portugal and meets Master Oliveira. The two men become fast friends.

It is in 1966 that the Master starts coming to Belgium and begins his teaching there that will carry on, two months a year, until his death in 1989. It is the Master who introduced his friend Antoine de Coux to our family.

I have named Antoine de Coux "the memory of the Master": passionate about horsemanship, passionate about the teachings of the Master, de Coux started to take notes at every clinic. Nothing can better characterize what he was than this excerpt of a letter, written in 1985 to Gerard Dufresne who was pushing him to publish his notes: "my notes help me follow the lessons in depth, and eventually relive them later. But I don't see how others could get some benefit from it, as you insist (except for some general reflections similar to the ones collected by Jeanne Boisseau). It would become "bookish" and hard to digest. *I am only the memory of the lived experience* [of Nuno Oliveira teachings]."

By the time of the Master's death, Antoine de Coux was finally convinced that he was in possession of an extraordinary patrimony, the "words of the Master" that was in need of being transmitted. He began the great labor of organizing his "notes" that he wrote in his lap [during the lessons], when he was not on a horse (let's not forget that he was himself an excellent *écuyer*).

Antoine de Coux died before finishing this extraordinary work. With the complete agreement of his daughter, inheritor of his manuscript,

---

2   [High school dressage trainer]

a team was constituted to finish the work.

The "notes" of Antoine are the reproduction of a spoken language. The punctuation represents the pause of the voice, the succession of the explanation, the chain of thought. The Master, who possessed an exceptional didactic talent, never hesitated to repeat the same things, but in a slightly different way. In order for the student to understand, he found a thousand turns of phrase to adapt them to his or her comprehension level. The "notes" of Antoine are the reflection of this preoccupation. Besides, we think that the repetition does "cadence" the reader's comprehension. We hope that he or she will feel as on a horse and will feel what to do or not to do [as if in a lesson with the Master].

By noting certain lessons from A to Z, and even reporting on the follow up of a certain horse over several days, Antoine de Coux added to the thoughts of general meaning or to the punctual pieces of advice, a lesson structure that illustrated perfectly the Master's science. He tells us to which degree he insisted on the action of the torso and reminds us of its finality, "ride by the thought alone," an expression that cannot be found in any of the great masters who preceded him.

At the home of Francis Laurenty, at Xhoris, three friends and écuyers leave the stable: Antoine de Coux (the Secretary of State), Nuno Oliveira (the Master), and Francis Laurenty (the driver).

Antoine de Coux, his gaze attentive and searching, his smile amiable and a little enigmatic.

At the top of one of his notebooks, Antoine de Coux wrote: "One of the great characteristics of the Master is that he is preoccupied by the physical and mental attitude of the horse rather than by performing movements." "Others" command the muscles of the horse. Nuno appeals to the mind of the horse and to his spirit of collaboration." He reproduces an excerpt of a conversation with some students (at the time, the Master was pushing Antoine to publish his "notes"): "There are enough books on the fundamental principles, but what doesn't exist is a compendium of notes 'lived' like these ones, which can develop the equestrian tact. Do they appear to be insignificant? To the contrary, I think that they are the ones that, on a horse, make you "feel." They include hundreds of comments, [representing dressage situations that] have been "lived." And I believe that I can affirm that a rider who would respect all those "details" would be a good rider.

Even if you do not have the stuff necessary to be a super champion, you wish to refine yourself and your sensations on a horse, to improve yourself. Don't lose sight of all those little pieces of advice.

What cannot be found in a book are the small remarks heard while one is on the horse (the value of which depends on the experience of he who gives them). I am giving you what cannot be found in [existing] books."

Could there be a better praise given to the work of Antoine de Coux?

The Master had read everything, experimented with everything, reflected on everything. He used to tell us often: re-read so-and-so, such and such page about…. But what he wanted to transmit to us was his anti-dogmatism, his sensitivity, his art. The "notes" of Antoine de Coux represent its best and final expression.

SUZANNE LAURENTY
Xhoris, Belgium, August 2006

THE TEAM:
Dr. Roger Bersoux
Sue, Miguel and Sara Oliveira
Catherine and Suzanne Laurenty
Students, friends, and their families.

It is not as strangers or as critics that we have looked into these "notes." We have every reason to want to entrust to future riders the teachings of an extraordinary Master, and to honor his "Secretary of State," as Antoine used to call himself.

16

GENERAL REMARKS

"For all the exercises, we must give the horse the clearest notion of what is being demanded from him. Long lasting impressions (which produce submission), are the result of correct actions, always the same. To speak clearly and simply and always in the same manner is one of the secrets of dressage."

Reflections on Equestrian Art
Nuno Oliveira

Rule: If the horse doesn't go forward, it is because there is too much hand. If he goes forward too much, it is because there is too much leg.

A poorly thought-out lesson (bad lateral work for instance, etc.) is bad for the horse's education. It teaches him to be defensive.

Dressage consists of bringing out the natural gaits of the horse.

There are two ways to do exercises:

1) The one that consists of forcing the horse to do them.

2) The one that consists of putting the horse first in the correct position and then giving him the maximum freedom to perform.

Never surprise the horse to obtain an exercise. Instead we must prepare and never snatch what we want.

Rule: ride your horse straight and ride him in the forward movement.

Importance and necessity of fixing the horse's head.

We often speak of the light hand, but not of the light leg. However, if the leg is hard, we send a contracted horse onto the hand.

Nuno Oliveira says: James Fillis has spoken of the domination of the horse. It is sometimes useful to provoke a fight, but don't start it if you don't have:

1) The capacity [to deal with the consequences] ,

2) The tenacity [to get to the end] and

3)The necessary seat [to stay on an unruly horse]. When we start a fight, we must be sure we are able to win.

A young horse may walk straight but be rigid. A horse can be straight and on the forehand, just like a piece of wood. [What we are seeking is a horse that] must be straight, but flexible rather than rigid, as supple in the left bend as in the right bend. One must feel the play of the

17

engaging hind leg. The hip must move slightly left when the left hind advances. Then the horse is straight in the good meaning of the word.

We must make an effort to have, perhaps less technique and more feeling.

The horse must be vigorous but remain calm.

What young riders who have never done "sport horsemanship" (jumping and cross-country) are missing is the sense of forward movement.

The geometry of the exercise disciplines the horse. [In a lesson,] it is neither recommended to always do the same work, nor to always do things in the same order.

If you ride the corners correctly[3], you get a more controlled horse.

If, once the lesson or the class is finished, you bring your horse back to the stable without anymore empathy than if you were parking your car in the garage, all [of what I am saying here] will not be of any interest for you.

Every time we change direction or go sideways, we must carefully choose the dose of aids we are using so the horse doesn't alter his cadence.

What is dressage? It is to train the horse so he becomes balanced (or find his balance again) with a rider on his back.

For each exercise, we need the positive tension, the vibration[4] adapted to this exercise. It is superior in trot than in walk, superior in flying changes every three strides than in flying changes every four strides. We must, in each exercise, maintain this positive tension until the end.

In the lesson it is useful to connect all the exercises together [and make them flow], without hiatus nor interruption.

We must not bring the horse back to the stable at the moment he is resisting.[5]

Advice to advanced riders. Often take the center-line–in the three gaits–to verify the results of your work and to see:
- If the horse is flexible.
- If the horse is straight.
- If the horse is in cadence.
- If the horse's position is maintained.

In the arena we must often use the center-line with the horse straight, because when we go along the wall we may have the illusion that all is well and we do not learn to go straight.

3   [Enter deeply and bend the horse with a hint of shoulder-in as recommended elsewhere by the Master]
4   [Nervous energy]
5   [Rather, we must end on a moment of peace and relaxation].

18

An example from the Master's (loaded) planner, and some associated notebooks.

Important rule:
- Ask often.
- Be happy with little.
- Stop at the right time.[6]
- Reward often.

The horse is a compass. He must "trace" the exercises correctly. The arena is a sheet of drawing paper.

A great principle for the entire conduct of dressage is to have the right dose, first of relaxation, and second, of the necessary energy. In fact, the horse is not a machine, but a living being. Therefore, we must know what dose of relaxation and degree of vigor that we must employ with each horse.

In equestrian art all the pretexts are good to "give," without abandoning the connection.

The main objective is to have balanced horses at the walk, trot and canter.

We must start every exercise with the best level of impulsion.

Starting right at the beginning of the training, we must look for the perfection of the simple exercises.

General rule: always put the horse in the correct position to perform the exercise requested.

6   [When the horse has produced his best for that day].

Do not force the horse to perform the exercises you want. Instead, prepare him to perform. Invite him to perform without forcing him. Try to obtain the exercises with the least aids possible. Try to obtain his collaboration, as a free horse and not as a slave. We must not work [ask for a new exercise, while] resistances are happening, but only ask for exercises based on the physical relaxation of the horse. To work well, it is better to be alone with your horse without spectators.

In a general sense (let it be for half-passes or pirouettes, etc.), the inside rein is used for the bend and the outside rein regulates everything else, by acting in parallel with the horse.

At a certain level, the rider must enter the world of sensations, meaning that he or she must try to feel the horse with his or her buttocks, back, hands, etc.. All this [is better done] without a "system" in the head.[7]

Technique is useful, even necessary, yet insufficient. Beyond [technique], we must feel and communicate with the horse.

We need technique, but we must also surpass it, get beyond it by the use of observation, reflection and by making an effort to understand what is going on in the horse's head.

There are some riders who only focus on technique. But we must also pay attention to sensations.

When the horse relaxes the jaw, he speaks to you, he is making conversation.

In dressage, the important things are the basics [impulsion, relaxation, straightness, roundness, etc.] otherwise we have to use all kind of artifice and tricks.

Note: Impress the beginning rider with the notion of creating forward movement without using force. It is a rule that suffers no exception (see the book: *Horses and their Riders*).[8]

"I want an energetic horse that is forward. However, my horsemanship is based on the physical and mental relaxation of the horse and the absence of force from the rider, because everything done with force contracts the horse. Collection is based on relaxation. If it is based on compression, it is no longer collection."

No complicated riding before the horses are truly going forward. In dressage, the difficulties are often created by a lack of good basic work (which is the "foundation of the house").

When a horse goes from one exercise to another, especially when he passes from canter to walk, we must not let [the horse] become "open" or lose his energy. We must therefore push him immediately forward.

7   [A dogmatic attitude that follows the rigid rules of a set progression prevents us from riding the horse as he is "in the moment"]

8   By Nuno Oliveira, *Oeuvres Complete*, published by Belin, 2006

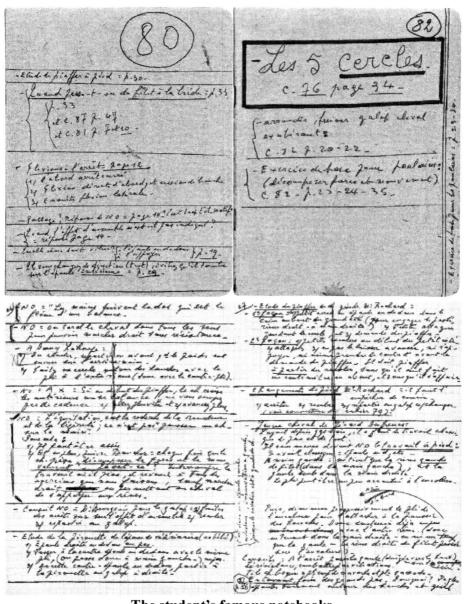

The student's famous notebooks.

A little teaching trick: to a rider who has constantly too much weight on the left rein in the work to the left and [whose horse] is never straight, Nuno Oliveira asks him to hold both reins in the right hand.

A yielding of the hand (*descente de main*), consists of ceasing to act

[with the hand] each time the horse is in balance.

When we stop the horse with the comprehensive action ("*effet d'ensemble*"):

1) Use the legs first and
2) Use the hands a fraction of a second later

To straighten a horse:

1) By [acting on] the forehand through using the outside rein [toward the neck if the horse is falling outward or away from the neck if the horse is falling inward].

2) Later, when the horse is trained and collected, we straighten him with the legs

Note: we must never hold the leg tight against the side. We must never use continuous aids, but rather, momentary aids[9].

In an exercise, it is often useful to go from the bend to the counter-bend.

When we take a diagonal [line to change rein], we must support the inside of the horse with the inside leg (fat of the calf) in relation to the center of the arena [for instance in a diagonal from left turn to right turn, use the left leg at the beginning of the diagonal and the right leg at the end]. Otherwise the horse will lean a little toward the inside of the arena, lose his straightness and a little bit of his impulsion.

Importance of the rider's torso: it is the "fulcrum of the scales." It can push, it can hold, according to the needs of the moment. It places weight forward or brings it back to the rear of the horse [in accordance with the rider's needs for better balance or more forward motion].

It is only when the horse is light that we can have delicate aids. [Our aids become progressively lighter in proportion to the horse increased lightness].

With a horse that holds himself back, we must push. But what to do with a horse that has a tendency to rush [and lose his balance]? In this case, lower the waist and, if your reins are adjusted to the right length and your elbows are in the right place, your reins will follow the [rebalancing] action of your torso [that will come up or even back]. Eventually, you can bring your outside shoulder back at the same time. In doing so you are working on the entire body of the horse. If you use only the reins, you will act on the mouth and the neck [not the body, which is the source of the problem].

The majority of riders' legs are too slow. To be able to use the legs quickly, they must be completely relaxed ("legs without bones") and well-placed [close to the horse without being glued to his sides].

Push – Take - Give

Push is to: -Engage the hind-end.

                     -Send the horse onto the hand.

                     -Create the connection.

---

9   [The exception is the leg pressure used for the "comprehensive effect" or "*effet d'ensemble*"]

Take is to:

-Prevent the horse from becoming "open" [lose his collection by disengaging the hind legs, flattening the back and pushing against the bit].

-Prevent the loss of the benefit of pushing.

-Stay short [collected] and round.

In brief, we shorten the horse from the back-end and we prevent him from opening.

Give is to:

-Reward.

-Lighten up the contact.

-Maintain the collection without a strong contact.

If the horse "opens" again, start again: push – take – give.

A short description of Equestrian Art:

1) Do a 6 meter volte at any gait, with the rider feeling equal sensations on both sides [of the horse]

2) With a correct position of the horse

3) With a good cadence

4) And with respect for the geometry of the exercise [round circle]

Many riders want to act like the boss all the time. Certainly, the rider must be able to "dominate his horse," but this is not needed all the time, rather it must be done "in the moment"[10]. The difficulty is to feel what dose [of authority] to use.

In equestrian art, it is easier to obtain [a movement] than to maintain.[11]

For one given horse, don't do everyday all he knows to do

Equitation [and dressage] is not a precise science, we must "feel."

In horsemanship, an important point is to decide:

-What is the dose of nervous energy is required of the horse?

-And what is the level of relaxation we must let him have?

There are two ways to lunge a horse:

-One consists in getting the horse tired.

-The other is used to create communication with the horse.

When the horse relaxes his jaw (but doesn't actually open his mouth), he is speaking to you, making conversation. If we consider equitation and dressage as merely a series of formulae, then it is not an art based on sensations [feeling].

---

10   [for a very short period, then give the horse a feeling of freedom again]

11   [The balance, the lightness, the cadence]

Chapter 1

EQUITATION, DRESSAGE, TACT

It is necessary for the horse to hold himself in a good position without being carried by the aids.

Dressage starts by the correct positioning (*placer*)[12] and the fixity of the head, by the *mise en main* (fixity and [the quality of a light] contact) and by the impulsion.[13]

It is not a good idea to work for a full hour in the *mise en main* [with the horse *ramené* and on the contact]. If we give [the hand] from time to time, we will get a connection that possesses a fresh quality when we take the contact up again. Importance of the fixity of the poll's position. If a horse lifts the poll when we start a new exercise, we lose the benefits of the previous exercise.

The horse must not have his head left or right or in the air [or too low]. Dressage outside of the *mise en main* [correct connection between the hand and the mouth] is without value. We need the poll to be in its correct place. And the fixity of the ensemble of the head and neck is indispensable [to good work].

It is right behind the [horse's] ears that we can observe if the poll is [correctly] flexed.

The degree of contact varies according to the horse and the rider, but if the poll is not flexed and the reins are abandoned, [it becomes] "trail riding" [not dressage].

[Following correctly] the geometry of the exercises disciplines the horse, creates a channel [for his movement]. Without [correctly ridden] exercises, the horse risks falling on one or the other shoulder.

Respect the discipline of the exercises: if a horse is crooked, he will lose his impulsion, he "floats.[14]"

There is no absolute in horsemanship. There are certainly some rules. But there is no "standard system." There are only principles.

A piece of advice: always keep your calm. Never get in a rage or

12   [which is a concept that includes *ramener*]

13   [As you will read in the chapter on the training of the young horse ("*debourrage*"), the dressage training as mentioned in this statement only starts after a period of riding the horse energetically forward on a loose rein].

14   [Oliveira uses the term 'float' in a negative sense. It means the horse is directionless, unguided, often crooked, and/or off the contact, and lacking impulsion.]

even become agitated, because you will then lose self-control and exceed the required measure.

Dressage is the development of movements that are slow and energetic.

Analyze less, feel more!

We must "feel," and not have a "system" in our head.

Prepare the exercise. It is important that nothing ever comes as a surprise for the horse.

Try to give the impression that everything you do is easy.

Never work for an hour without rewarding, without calming [the horse]. Walk [frequently] on a loose rein.

Do your best so the horse enjoys the movement.

Every corner of the arena is a little piece of shoulder-in.

Don't start an exercise without the correct degree of impulsion.

The difficult side of the horse doesn't necessarily need to be worked for more time, but rather with more attention [to detail], ridden more delicately. It is not by working for a long time that the problems get taken care of, but by paying attention to the appropriateness of the aids.

We must not exaggerate the bend, except momentarily to overcome a resistance.

Something fundamental: physical and mental relaxation. Don't start anything without it.

To resolve a problem, we need technique. But that doesn't suffice. It must be completed by thought and by feeling. If we only have technique, [the result] is sad.

Equestrian tact consists notably of anticipating the moment when a horse will lose impulsion. Afterwards, it is already too late.

The brain of the rider must "go down into his seat."

We must not stay too long in one exercise.

Academic equitation is the research of accuracy in:
1) The study of cadence.
2) The use of the aids.
3) The symmetry of the exercises.

The first thing to do: get the horse to accept discipline and get him "in impulsion."[15]

The criteria of a good rider: is a rider that we cease to notice, and we only watch the horse.

The best judge to appreciate the quality of the rider's aids is the

---

15   [A fundamental concept in all of Nuno. Oliveira's work].

horse. Look at his attitude, his ears, his eye [they tell the truth by their expression].

If the rider who just won a dressage class dismounts and his horse has a miserable appearance, we can say that the rider is a savage. The work was some kind of sport, and not equestrian art.

Many riders are disappointed by explanations that are simple and logical. They would rather hear very scholarly explanations instead.

Dressage consists of finding a way to get the horse to employ himself to the maximum in the chosen exercise and then maintain the work without the help of the aids. A trained horse is a supple horse, pleasant to ride, happy, and not a horse that gesticulates.

Dressage must be practiced with the constant preoccupation of [placing sufficient] weight on the hind-end [to achieve a good balance], but without grabbing the mouth.

We must feel the jaw of our horse. Horsemanship is a dialogue between the hand and the jaw.

Please read the *"Dialogues on Equitation"* by François Baucher [Xenophon Press *François Baucher: The Man and His Method* 2012].

We must work not only on the physique of the horse, but also the mental, the mind of the horse. And during that work, we must catch his attention.

Horsemanship is, for certain riders, a partnership with the horse, for others, it is an hour of wrestling, a sheer brawl.

We must be perfectionists in the [application of the] details and in the [understanding of the] basic principles.

Rule: the lowering of the neck must happen softly and only when the rider asks for it. It is not the horse that must pull the reins off from the rider's hands.

Horses have their favorite spots in the arena (*querencia*[16] in Portuguese). We must make the most of it [when we choose where to start an exercise, particularly a new exercise that the horse is learning].

The lateral bend: it is important at first to get the horse to move sideways in balance [leg yielding] and then, the bend will develop [progressively]. Don't obsess about the bend at the start of training. At the beginning what is important, is the lateral push of the hind legs rather than the bend (particularly in half-passes).

We must not ask an old horse to perform everything he knows how to do and is able to do.

Clearly we must put the horse in discipline. However, we must avoid trying to dominate him all the time, otherwise he will brace himself.

---

16   haunts

When we use force to train horses, they become numb. Besides, they are much stronger than we are.

When we ask for a new movement from the horse (the first flying change for instance), it is a good idea to finish the lesson with exercises of calm and relaxation.

We should be suspicious of big, rapid progress. Small daily progress is much preferable.

Force under the purpose of firmness can only be used for a fraction of a second.

We must always insist on a supple horse and in the study of new exercises and concepts, one must go progressively.

Equestrian tact consists of feeling when the horse will lose his impulsion and prevent this [from happening]. It is acting at the right moment, in small doses and adequately.

We can resolve problems either:

1) By staying in the gait we are in [at the moment when the problem arises],

2) Or, more often, by returning to walk.

The first solution, [above] best suits a horse that is not very generous and would have a tendency to fall asleep at the walk.

The second solution best suits a horse with a more lively temperament and would have a tendency to become nervous if forced to stay in the gait [in which the problem arose].

It is not the audience that we must impress and seduce, but, quite to the contrary, the horse.

Equestrian art begins with the perfection of simple things.

If your horse becomes nervous, *you* must stay calm at all costs.

The good ending of the last lesson becomes the preparation of the next one and is reflected in its quality.

The beauty of dressage is to see a horse who, without looking sleepy, gives the impression of working without effort.

I don't like people who say: "my horse already does this and that." What is needed is a relaxed horse that walks straight, who is light. The horse deserves consideration. He has served mankind for centuries. He has helped make the history of the world. He deserves respect and not only to be used by people as a pedestal.

Advice to the instructors: in your lessons, never ask from a horse, or a rider, what they are incapable of doing.

Many riders practice dressage without having truly galloped or jumped [on a race track or cross country] and, as a result do not know what forward movement really is.

A trained horse can be stopped from the canter without the use of the reins (as if they had been suddenly cut off).

The ideal in horsemanship is to do the exercises while maintaining the horse round and in physical and mental relaxation, with the rider [apparently] doing nothing at all. It is not an "abandoned horse" but a horse in balance [ridden with invisible aids].

If there is no relaxation of the mouth, it is not possible to have lightness.

What we commonly name "dressage" [as in the modern sport discipline] *on one hand and "Equestrian Art" on the other, are two different things.*

The current problem is that so many people teach equitation without knowing how to ride themselves.

To connect the exercises, it is important to prepare each of one of them and not surprise the horse.

It is very important to maintain the fixity of the poll [to prevent its raising in the transitions].

A principle: to create the conditions for the horse to perform the exercise, we must prepare him.

A straight horse is not the exclusive result of a visual approach [the horse looks straight because the] (head, neck, ears, etc.) [aligned], but also [making] the horse symmetrical and straight in the sensations [he gives to the rider], with no more weight on one shoulder than the other and the feeling that one is sitting in the axis [of the horse].

When we mention a "straight horse," it's not only the shoulders and haunches which must be in the same line [in the longitudinal plane], but also the ears must be at the same height and without the head tilted.

Under the pretext of relaxing [the horse], we must not let the impulsion die. We must stay vigilant and, eventually, "liven up" the impulsion again.

We must feel [the movement of] the back of the horse.

Often what is taught is not untrue. But they are "clichés," correct [when applied to] trained horses, but not necessarily true with a specific individual horse at a particular stage of training. It is not adapted [to the reality of training at that moment]; it is just theory.

The equestrian tact does not consist exclusively of the delicacy of the aids, but also in the choice of the aids used. And it is also in the smoothness of the aids as a whole.

Many horses present special [training] cases, and in each of these cases, we must feel what to do, which aids to use: It is all about equestrian tact.

The Germans prefer to give the horse the precision of a machine.

I prefer to give him all the brilliance he is capable of.

Remembering Baucher: "In the end, we always come back to Baucher: decomposing the force and the movement. How do we achieve that? By doing all the exercises we know but without ever letting the horse walk straight while he resists."

We must deduce from reading Baucher (between the lines) that he warns us against the diagonal effects used in exaggeration or prematurely.

Baucher again: "ask often, be happy with a little bit, reward a lot."

Walk Pirouette

In the walk pirouette, we must alternate the action of the legs so the hind feet of the horse don't get stuck.

When can we go from the simple snaffle to the double bridle?

When the horse doesn't resist against the snaffle, doesn't move his head and is truly forward. The main rule is to feel what suits him best. Before putting a double bridle [in his mouth], the horse must be [connected and] *ramené* [the horse "in the hand" with the forehead on the vertical] on a snaffle.

When can we begin using the "effet d'ensemble"? [17]

When the horse is truly forward, when he accepts the spur and is relaxed in his head.

The half-pirouette in trot:

Nuno tells us that this is not easy to do. We must put the horse in trot as if he was getting into piaffe. It is an exercise of "La Guérinière's Square." It must be done nearly in piaffe. In fact, in high equitation, it is actually done in piaffe.

[Preparing] *the pirouette in canter:*

1) In walk at X, do some small circles in shoulder-in
[for example shoulder-in right on the right circle]
2) In walk at X, small circles around the haunches
[for example, haunches-in right on the right circle]
3) In walk at X, small circles in counter-shoulder-in on the other hand [for example, on the small circle to the left, shoulder-in right]
4) In walk at X, after 2 or 3 steps of [right] counter-shoulder-in [on the left circle], depart into the [right] canter pirouette

---

17   [Effect on the whole or comprehensive effect: legs and hands acting together].

(back to the original hand) [turning right].

The purpose of the few steps in counter-shoulder-in, is to avoid the natural tendency of the horse to lean to the inside of the pirouette.

Contact:

1) With a young horse, work the horse in the forward motion, keep him relaxed and do not worry about the tension of the reins at that stage.

2) Progressively, the horse becomes impulsive and engages the haunches.

3) Later, if the horse reaches a superior form of impulsion (which is rare), he will be able to work in "half tension" [when the reins alternate between light contact and a slight slack during the stride].

We must concern ourselves with the back before the *ramené* of the head and neck of the horse. It is the back that must show the [positive] tension.[18]

What is the contact?

It is only in particular cases that we must act with the hands alone by "division of contact"[19], by "vibrations"[20] and *"badinages"*[21], etc.. But in general, contact is regulated, not by the hand independent of the torso, but by the hand accompanying the torso's movements, with the elbows resting on the rider's hips, from which we see the importance of the role of the rider's torso [and of its actions].

When it becomes more erect, the torso loads the hind-end and, in doing so, facilitates the engagement of the hind legs[22].

Then the hand receives what the hind-end sends towards it. This is the true contact. Therefore, we must always start by the seat [acting towards] a fixed hand. It is only after [this is assured] that we can use some small complementary actions of the hand.[23]

<u>A horse</u> with a "mute" mouth[24] is not light. It is also useful to watch

18   [This means that the superficial back muscles are relaxed and the spine is slightly raised].

19   [A technique of Baucher in which the rider holds the snaffle rein on the inside of the bend and the curb on the outside, while dropping the contact of the other two reins]

20   [An action in which the entire forearm shakes very fast in a limited range of motion]

21   [Wiggling of the fingers while the arm doesn't move]

22   [This works well as long as the rider sits in the front of the saddle and the saddle itself is equipped of wide panels that are comfortable to the horse's back]

23   [Nuno used to say that the contact was created 95% by the seat and 5% by the hand]

24   [A mouth with an immobile tongue and jaw that doesn't respond to the solicitation of the hand]

31

the ears: if they never point forward and are always turned back, it is a bad sign.

Actions of the hand that go from down to up are clearly better than actions that go from front to back (the correct movement is similar to the one used to raise a spoon to the mouth).

It is better to risk losing a little contact than to not give.

We must have the sensation that the neck of the horse is in front of the hands; for this to happen, we must adjust the reins correctly.

With a trained horse, position the horse and let him perform. (Position without [continuous] action [of the aids]).

At Francis Laurenty's stable, Antoine leans on the railing, taking notes.

Chapter 2

POSITIONS, AIDS

The academic position is the only one that permits the use of light aids.

When the horse trots, it is not necessary for the "steels" (bits and spurs) to also trot.

Make yourself light on the horse's back. The rider is light when he is relaxed and doesn't oppose himself to the movement. It means to be in unity with the horse .

We must prepare the horse, not surprise him.

If you compress the legs, you will receive a heavy horse on the hand. They provoke the rigidity of the horse and also contract the body of the rider.

All the pretexts are good to do a *descente de main* [yielding/lowering/relaxing of the hand]. Do it as often as possible. Nevertheless, do not give *(descente de main)* before the horse is light, otherwise the horse is in a vacuum [connection will be lost].

If necessary, act with the spurs of course. But it is not by the spur that the horse is made to go but by the action of the seat well-accorded with the horse.

It is essential to feel if the spur touches or not[25].

Important rule: independence of the legs [in relation to each other]. We must manage, when we use one leg that the other one doesn't become stuck [against the other side], [the leg that is not acting] must not move, in short, remains independent of what the other is doing.

By moving the legs in the trot, we upset its cadence.

"Take and give," but not taking nor giving too much. What is needed is to take in the moment, that is the secret.

The [rider's] heels must not be too high or too low [by compressing or opening the ankle's angle too much in either direction]. Otherwise it becomes ugly and it always a contraction of the ankles.

To ride without the aids, it's not to abandon the horse, is to keep the connection while acting as little as possible.

The continuous actions of the legs push the horse out of rhythm.

---

25   [and also to be able to maintain a constant and even pressure for the time needed to perform an *effet d'ensemble* – comprehensive effect]

The continuous use of the spur renders the horse indifferent or makes him nervous.

It is only with a good position that the rider can be free of his movements, of his aids. It is only the academic position that renders possible the independence and the delicacy of the aids.

Learn to ride without the aids.

Every action of the hand must be preceded by an action of the legs. Every time the horse resists, reinforce the academic position, therefore bring the torso back, and close the fingers after an action of the legs. The action of the legs must precede [the hands], otherwise the horse lifts the head, hollows the loins instead of engaging the hind legs. In the "comprehensive effect" ["*effet d'ensemble*" as Baucher names it, "*action d'ensemble*" as Oliveira names it], the actions of the legs must also slightly precede the actions of the hands.

The rider's legs must push from back to front and not the opposite. Therefore slightly turn the toes to the outside.

The advantage of keeping the legs close [to the sides]:

1) at the moment of action, we don't surprise the horse

2) and we act quicker because we don't have to move the legs prior [to the action].

Don't contract the legs nor glue them to the horse, but don't swing them continuously either. The horse gets used to it and falls asleep, like we fall asleep with the tick-tock of a clock. It is better to guess when the impulsion will wane and then act: a little tap, sharp and quick with a relaxed leg or if needed, a sharp little hit with the spur.

It is not the inside of the knee that must touch the horse, because if the inside is in contact, the [belly of the] calf can't touch. It is the hollow of the back of the knee ["*creux poplite*"] that must be in contact and the belly of the calf that caresses softly [the side of the horse]. We must embrace the horse, wrap [the legs] around as if we were sitting on a barrel. Have as many points of [very light] contact as possible.

"Each part of the [rider's] body must rest on the part that is below it." - François Baucher

The comprehensive effect ["*action d'ensemble*"] is an action of the hands and the legs acting together. The legs send [the horse] onto a hand that controls, but a soft hand. The torso also plays its role by getting taller and the waist by advancing towards the hand.

While cantering on a volte or a circle to the right, look to the right toward the center of the circle. Therefore the left shoulder advances a little bit with a slight turn of the torso toward the right. Also place the weight on the right, load the right stirrup a little.

34

Many horses are special cases [that don't fit in the usual progression of dressage described in classical books] and in each of these cases, we must feel what to do, which aids to use. It is the [domain] of *equestrian tact.*

Humans have slower reflexes than horses, so they must practice the quickening of their reflexes. For instance, to make a "correction," the intervention must be quick, in the moment and in the place [of the arena the problem happened], but measured in the right dose and instantaneous. [Meanwhile, keep] great softness in between [corrections].

If the horse is performing the exercise well, we must diminish the aids a little, even cease to use them. The horse must carry on with the movement on his own, which doesn't mean [for the rider] to "abandon" [the horse].

In principle, the hands must always stay at the same height. However, in order to create bend (half-pass, canter on the circle, etc.), it is necessary to "wrap" [the neck] with the outside rein, which may be placed a little higher than the other one. If needed, like when driving a car, [the hands] can move within the limits of the [rider's] shoulder displacement.

The rider's leg must be neither forward nor backward (except in some particular [training] cases), but simply "dropped down" [in their natural place].

Hands: must be like concrete if the horse resists (but with a FIXED hand and not with a hand that pulls).

The comprehensive effect: it may require [occasionally] hands of concrete, but also needs the rider to stretch the torso upward [and advance the waist] in order to push the hind-end forward with the seat.

Often the hands move [uncontrollably] because the lower back is not relaxed.

To dominate the horse: play with the reins (with a delicate movement and without pulling).

We must have an immobile hand with mobile fingers that opens and closes (but need to close only rarely with a trained horse).

"Long legs" doesn't mean legs placed backwards. It is the rider's thigh that must be as straight and vertical as possible,[26] with the knee dropped.

When we use a *rein of opposition*[27] we must use it close to the base of the neck. When we use such a rein near the middle of the neck, it is broken[28].

Don't have "rule book hands," rigid, with the fingers tensed for-

26   [within the constraints of each rider's anatomy]
27   [closest concept to the neck rein in American riding]
28   [create a false flexion in the wrong place of the neck]

ward, but natural, relaxed hands, wrists included.

The *lateral aids* (to be used with young horses) [help the horse] to extend, while the diagonal aids engage [the hind legs] and sit [the horse].

One of the [most important] *secrets* of riding is the [correct] "dosage" between legs and hands, [the "accordance of the aids"].

In canter, if the rider does not move very much, the horse achieves cadence more easily.

Arms and legs must be independent of the torso. Everything below the waist must be independent of everything above it.

Importance of the softness of the waist when it moves forward, especially to avoid [undue] movements and vertical shocks.

When we bring the torso or the waist back, the legs must not move forward.

Think about the dosage of the hand in relation to the dosage of the legs. It is the [fundamentally important] "accord of the aids."

The beginning of the hand is the shoulder. The beginning of the leg is the hip.

As much as possible, replace the actions of hands and legs by actions of the torso.

In the canter, it is the horse that "*bascules*" [the specific rocking back and forth motion of the horse in canter and during a jump] and not the rider.

We must decide on the length of rein that suits each and every horse.

We must feel [rather than analyze] what we need to do.

In order not to surprise the horse, we need to use the hand as a "follower" of the torso. The elbows placed near the rider's torso (resting on our hips), *the hands follow the mouth by the play of the rider's back*[29].

Use the tightening of the fingers, but never pull the hand back[30].

In the loops of the walk serpentines, pay attention that the horse keeps the same contact on the right rein as on the left rein. This is the proof that the horse has not "broken" his neck [taken an excessive bend in one location or another].

To perform a serpentine, the seat and the shoulders [of the rider] suffice.

In a serpentine, before finishing one loop, we must already think about the next one.

[To achieve] the suppleness of [the horse's] back, never bring the shoulders back without the waist advancing.

29   [and not by an independent action that follows the neck. This is the definition of the FIXED HAND]

30   [another fundamental aspect of the FIXED HAND]

Do not hang on the reins, instead, treat them like silk ribbons, as ornaments of the horse's neck.

One example of the usefulness [of the controlled disposition] *of the rider's weight*: it is very useful in changing from the shoulder-in to the half-pass. In effect, at the end of the shoulder-in, the weight is placed on the outside (to the right in the left shoulder-in). To transition from the shoulder-in to the half-pass after the corner, we will displace the rider's weight from right to left.

Remarks on the position: The most important part of the back is not its highest section, but the part that goes from the middle of the back all the way down to the knee.

Also, in relation to the legs, the hands have a different role. We often forget that it is the legs, (small of the back included) that push the horse forward to the hand, and that the hands' role is only to channel this force by using very discreet rein aids.

In the volte for instance, we must not act through great efforts of the reins but by using the legs.

If the horse leans inward in the volte, it is the legs that must intervene, in particular the inside leg to create bend.

In conclusion, the [main] quality of the leg is effectiveness and the [main] quality of the hand is discretion.

To collect, don't quibble: reinforce the academic position, use the legs to send the horse to a soft [fixed, restraining] hand (*action d'ensemble*) [comprehensive effect]. The legs send the horse to a controlling hand, but a soft hand. The torso plays its part by becoming more erect and the waist acts by advancing toward the hand.

The hands. Avoid having "wandering" hands. They must move only within the limits of the swinging of the shoulders that they are accompanying.

The fact of being able to keep the sole of the boot in contact with the thread of the stirrup is one proof that the leg does not lift [uncontrollably].

To turn, advance the outside shoulder a little and use a soft pressure of the inside leg near the girth.

The hands must not come closer to the body, it is the body that must come close to the hands. Without the shoulders coming back!

When the hands act, it is not from front to back but from lower to higher.

Don't act all the time, but keep the aids in the position [appropriate] for requesting, so we can intervene without undue delay.

Don't flex the wrists outwards, instead, round them with the hands [knuckles] facing each other.

Don't abandon the horse but [use] as little aids as possible. We must get the horse used to function without being "carried" by the rider. He must keep himself in balance [self-carriage]. To achieve this goal, he must become relaxed and he cannot be rushed [pushed too hard] or compressed. He must hold himself in a good position, without being carried by the aids but by his own effort.

More than 50% of the rider's success in dressage, [results from] his or her position. The rider's position on a horse is everything, as long as it is a relaxed position (a body [nearly] without muscles, like an old fashioned "stuffed doll"). It is only with a good position that the rider can be free to move and to "aid" as needed. Only the academic position makes possible the independence and the delicacy of the aids.

Make sure the branches [shanks] of the bit sit in the horse's mouth symmetrically. If we see the branches of the bit move, it is because the hand is not properly fixed [in relation to the horse's back].

If the action of the hand is not accompanied with an action of the torso, it only influences the head of the horse. However, it is necessary that the hind-end of the horse move to "meet" the horse's mouth.

At the walk, don't mess with the reins: adjust them to the correct length, then regulate the speed with your torso. And after that, let him walk.

If at the trot the hands of the rider also "trot," it is proof that his or her waist is rigid.

Act little but in the right amount, instantaneously, in the moment. A stronger action, a few seconds late, is less effective.

The channel or corridor of the aids.
To the right: right hand and right leg.
To the left: left hand and left leg.
For example, to bend the horse in the volte: the inside leg and hand bend and the outside hand and leg "wrap around," channeling the horse.

Rule: don't act with autonomous [independent] hands, but use the torso with fixed hands that follow the torso, elbows resting on the points of the hips.

The foundation of the rider is his or her torso, his or her accessories: arms and legs.

What is a *descente de main et de jambs* [yielding of the hand and leg aids]? It is when the aids cease their action[31].

---

31   [and release without abandoning the horse]

Sitting is not being static, it is feeling what is happening in the back of the horse. We must feel that the entire body of the horse "gets up" to the hand, ending up in what is in his mouth and remains stable[32].

It is not enough that the fingers are relaxed; we also need our wrists to be relaxed and not rigid.

Recommendation: pay particular attention to acquiring [a sufficient] speed of reflexes = instantaneous actions of hands and legs (without brutality!).

When riding, we must not initiate movements of the torso; it is the horse that makes movements and creates our own.

The more relaxed the legs [of the rider] are, the more relaxed the horse is. The less relaxed the legs are, the less relaxed the horse is.

The hand must not move, but it must not fall asleep, and become inert. The subtlety of your hand must feel the vibrations that occur in the horse's head.

Make a habit of stroking the horse when he has "given himself" and has done something well.

Position: try to maintain–without effort the vertical torso, (neither forward nor backward) and the waist well relaxed.

Do not tense nor lift the shoulders, but keep them relaxed.

Act little, but appropriately, in the moment.

The spur constantly glued to the horse does not teach the horse to go forward but, on the contrary, gets him used to holding back.

Contracted legs contract the horse as much as the rider.

Don't [use] labored aids, do little.

Always precede the actions of the hands by an adjustment of the torso, that fits the sensations coming from the horse's back. The reins must be adjusted at the correct length.

Tension of the reins [when needed] doesn't imply heaviness [of the hands].

Don't depart into trot with loose reins.

The hand is neither a cork[33] nor a faucet[34], but a filter[35].

The good trot is the trot in which the horse maintains the same position of the poll, the same speed, the same cadence, with the same intensity of contact.

Increasing the impulsion of the walk does not consist of getting more speed, but more energy.

32   [fixed head position, constant height of the poll]
33   [that stops the flow of energy]
34   [that lets it all escape]
35   [that controls its debit]

During the entire life of the horse, take and give and never block.

When we transition from a higher gait into an lower one (for instance from trot to walk), we must push in order for the horse to begin the new gait with impulsion.

Hold the reins as if they were made of silk threads. It is not leather that you are holding in your hands but sheer silk.

Push [the horse] with your back; slow [the horse] down with your back, without moving your hands.

Advice to verify the cadence of the trot: close your eyes and count 1-2-1-2.

In a turn, the horse turns around the inside leg.

Tighten the fingers to vanquish a resistance, open them to reward [the horse].

[When dealing with a resistance], fix the fingers convulsively on an immobile hand (that doesn't go back even 1 millimeter). That is not pulling! Give when the horse gives in and collects himself.

When you touch the horse with the spur, don't scare him.

The hand cannot be fixed if the buttocks are not glued to the saddle and those cannot be glued if the waist is not relaxed.

A heavy rider can be light on the horse and a small rider can be heavy on the horse.

Always be scared of pulling but never be scared of pushing.

In the trot, make the circle smaller with the outside rein. Make the circle larger with the inside rein.

A good thing for beginners is to always rest the hands on the withers.

When you feel the horse becoming round, hold the reins in semi-tension.

If, in a session of lateral work, you carry on using your aids after the horse has given:

1) you upset the cadence

2) you confuse the horse who doesn't understand that he has done the right thing because you keep insisting on demanding [for more lateral action].

Don't let the horse fall asleep on the obsession of a fixed contact [on a fixed but lifeless hand].

The inside rein is for beginner riders [and beginner horses]. The outside rein (acting upward) is for advanced riders [and educated horses].

The principal aids are the seat and the torso. Hands and legs are secondary aids.

The spurs have a lot less virtues than one thinks.

If the hands intervene independently from the torso, we only affect the head and neck.

If in the circle (in trot for instance), you use too much inside rein, you may break the neck and the horse has a tendency to place his quarters to the outside.

Your legs must be like two walls and your horse will work in a corridor ["the channel of the aids"].

To fix [the hand] is not pulling, it is adjusting [the reins] and keeping quiet.

Place your hands in an "easy" position, with relaxed wrists, not like a "fashion picture."

In the turns of the trot serpentine, sit on the inside, load the inside stirrup.

Don't be attached to the mouth of the horse; maintain a light contact.

When we ask the horse to cut ["*doubler*"] the arena (at A for instance to go on the center line), the speed must remain constant.

We can collect (at the walk for example) a horse who is marching too quickly: we need [to establish] the appropriate walk [to create collection].

When riding, it is useful to sometimes close our eyes.

Superiority of the legs over the hand:

In trot for instance, enter a corner by an action of the inside leg (the two reins being kept at the same length), rather than by the action of the inside rein. This [action] will improve the quality of the trot. [By the same logic] In a circle at the canter, when making the circle smaller or larger, the action of the leg (outside leg to make the circle smaller and inside leg to make it larger) should be superior to the action of the hand on the same side. The delicate point is to know which dose of the leg action is appropriate to use.

Nuances of the use of the leg:

1. The inside leg must always be rubbery and pleasant, never hard.

2. Also remember that the use of the leg is not limited to tapping with the heel but that the leg can also be employed at different heights starting with the hip of the rider.

3. It is more useful to use a little movement of the hip or of the fattest part of the calf than the bottom of the leg [heel or spur]. This little movement of the hip can harmonize our weight with the movement of the

41

horse.

Example: On the left rein, lower the left hip before leaving the wall to take the diagonal.

When too much aids [are being used] it is no longer equitation, it is forcefulness.

Keep the contact (a light contact) with well-adjusted reins. If they are too short you diminish the impulsion; if they are too long, the horse floats and you are abandoning him.

We must be light on the back of the horse: the rider is light when he's relaxed, does not have a rigid torso, nor contracted buttocks. A rigid torso is contrary to the movement. It is noticeably the case when the rider puts his/her shoulders too far back.

Position on Horseback:

1. Embrace the horse with the back of the knee as if you were sitting on a barrel.

2. Have the same turning out of the toes as in the ordinary walk [meaning the rider's walk].

3. Do not bring the elbows back, nor place the hand backwards anywhere on the abdomen.

4. Lower the thighs while keeping the heels in the vertical of the rider's neck.

5. Keep all joints supple [relaxed].

6. Lower the shoulders.

7. [Push] the belly-button towards the ears of the horse.

8. The back of the buttocks must not go behind the vertical line of the shoulders.

9. Coccyx[36] [pushed] toward the pommel of the saddle.

We must be at one with the horse otherwise he doesn't understand what we want. Therefore do not hang on the reins, nor push on the stirrups, but simply be seated with the fat of the calves in a soft contact [with the sides]. It is the fat of the calf that must be in contact.

The Hand:

The thumb and the forefinger must be closed on the reins, and it must be the other three fingers, (the pinky, the ring finger and the middle finger) that play and give.

Position of the Hands:

We must search for the place (in a small space) where the horse

---

36   A small triangular bone forming the lower extremity of the spinal column in humans.

accepts the hands in the easiest way and where the rider is most at ease.

The legs should be near the horse's flanks, but without squeezing, soft and without force.

Don't lift the shoulders up because it contracts them. The beginning of the rider's hand is the shoulder.

(Nuno Oliveira) to a certain rider: "Your horse has a considerable lateral mobility. You must be very attentive to frame him [in the corridor of the aids] otherwise he will float."

Legs: When the legs must act, it should be by touches not by pressure or squeezing.

If the waist is rigid, it can't accompany [the horse's movement] and the hands will move [uncontrollably].

If the legs are tight or far away [from the sides], they cannot act immediately, in the moment that they are needed.

The principle is to be linked with the movement of the horse with some exceptions. For instance, if the horse rushes we can oppose [our seat motion to his increase in tempo]. Therefore, in principle, it is good to place our shoulders parallel to the shoulders of the horse, except when he rushes.

An Exercise to Improve the Riders Position:

Standing with the back to the wall, (and the feet slightly away from the wall), lower the knees while maintaining the back of the head against the wall and pushing the hips forward as you go down. Get back up in the reverse way.

Hierarchy of the aids:

1. First [act with] the torso and the waist of the rider.

2. And only then use the hands and the legs.

The mistakes of the legs are paid for in the mouth. When the rider says that his horse rushes, it is often when there has been an overuse of the legs.

The legs give and take as the hand does, but not by being tight. The waist can also give and take.

When the horse gives, it is necessary that the rider also gives. Otherwise, in the majority of cases the horse will end up resisting even more.

For example, after a medium trot, we can take by using the waist instead of using the hands.

When the rider contracts the legs, he also contracts other parts of his body (torso, etc.) and he receives a rigid horse on his hands.

43

In the case of flying changes, or for all other exercise, prepare rather than surprise your horse.

Each action of the rider's hand must be preceded by an adjustment of the torso.

Yielding or giving is not abandoning, it is seizing the action. And fixing [the hand] is not pulling.

Series of Advice Given to Intermediate Riders of a Riding School.
1. Pushing is not squeezing the legs; it is touching (with the legs). If you squeeze, you contract your entire body and you transmit this contraction to the horse.

2. Don't forget that the waist can also slow down as well as push [the horse].

Wait until the horse places [his head on the vertical] through the exercise and the effect of the cadence, rather than by the action of the hands.

To a student working in the trot: The more you use your hands, the more the horse arches his neck and the less he engages his hind legs.

To another student: You are forced to use your hands a lot because your legs are glued [to the sides of the horse]. You are contracting your horse.

In the trot: If you have too much inside rein, you break [the neck at its base] and you take the impulsion away.

To a student trotting to the right: if you have too much right rein, the head is too much to the right and he pushes his left shoulder to the outside.

Every time the rider uses his or her hands too strongly, one induces the horse into a fight.

Relax your hands, so the horse feels less jammed. Let him use his neck more.

If a horse wants to lift his head, close the fingers a fraction of a second without the hand moving back. The action must be quick in order to get ahead of the movement of the head.

If a horse becomes over-bent, use small vibrations with an upward motion, but very softly.

When you are doing a straight line on the diagonal, look in that direction.

If your horse is not light, do everything you want (voltes, etc.), but don't do anything sudden (like a short halt for instance), because that would contract him physically and mentally and you would lose the benefit of your work.

If the horse has a resistant side, play on the reins on the resistant side and try your best to keep the contact on the other side (because horses have a tendency to avoid the contact on the side opposite to their resistance). The more you fight on the resistant side, the more he is going to resist. You must relax the hand on the resistant, difficult side.

Before playing with the reins[*pianoter les rênes*], you must abandon [the contact] a little bit. We must not play [*pianoter*] on a tight rein. The play must not reduce the impulsion.

We must push [the horse forward, not necessarily for speed but to create the direction of the impulsion from back to front] because to place [the horse's head vertically], impulsion [is necessary] .

[Immediately] after pushing on a fixed hand, play on the rein with the fingers, because a fixed hand doesn't mean fixed and rigid fingers.

The Academic position is taught in [many] books. But according to the sensations [we receive from the horse], we must make room for nuances. To be always upright can be a sign of rigidity and ineffectiveness. What is really important is to have a torso that is adaptable [in all circumstances]. We must put our body in accord with the movement of the horse.

For the rider's hand, let's remember the frequently used comparison of the open faucet, the cork and the filter.

It is easy to yield. What is difficult is to take again *after* a yielding [of the hand].

Nuno Oliveira shows a student how to take with the torso (he places his finger on the student's kidneys) [to insist on his suppleness].

The more a horse is on the forehand, and the more cautious we must be about using the hand [to remedy the problem]: it is with the torso and the weight of the body that we must act.

If you bring the shoulders back without relaxing the waist, you detract from the impulsion. It is therefore necessary to soften and advance the waist rather than keep the loins rigid. It is the movement of the waist forward which must bring the shoulders back.

The legs must remain independent from each other. When we act with one leg, it is necessary that the other one is able to remain quiet.

One of the favorite sentences of the Master: "The more we do, the less it works; the less we do, the better it works."

Rule: act little but in the moment.

For the execution of an exercise, the intensity of the aids must diminish progressively as the horse enters the exercise and surrenders to it. I am trying to say that if the horse executes the exercise as of his own volition, the aids must be reduced.

We close the fingers to vanquish a resistance, we open them to reward.

It is the outside rein that maintains the collection [*rassembler*] in the canter.

During the entire life of the horse, and at any time: [it is needed]

1)Hands : take and give:

– Take = tighten the fingers as he resists and [give:] softens them as soon as he yields.

Therefore, [we practice] yielding of the hand [*descente de main*] all the time.

2) Legs: intervention every time there is a risk of losing the impulsion.

Descente de main [yielding of the hand]:

The rider opens the hand (loosens the fingers) and the horse must keep the same position, the same cadence, the same gait. The yielding of the hand is not doing a particular gesture, but simply "not acting" with the hand, ceasing to act. We must always have a subtle hand. Ceasing is not acting, but it is not abandoning the horse.

Effet d'ensemble [comprehensive effect]

Action of the hands and legs together. It is a call to order. It must always be followed by a cession of hands and legs.

Effet d'ensemble: the horse halted with the spurs in contact near the girth. This must become a conditioned reflex for the horse: the [light, constant, even pressure] of the spurs in this area of his body means halt and tranquility. To start forward movement again: use the spurs further back on the horse.

Never act with the hands before acting with the legs: every action of the hand must be preceded by an action of the leg. The action of the legs does not necessarily mean an action of the calves because the leg of the rider starts at the hip. The leg must act from the top towards the bottom. From this stems the fact that it will often suffice for the leg to act, the rider will only need to sit down more.

It is the loins (supple, soft and not stiff) of the rider which have the most important role; they must dominate the horse. It is with the buttocks that we push the horse forward. The shoulders must not swing [come forward and backward without control] nor the loins stay fixed; on the contrary :the [rider's] shoulders must be fixed and the loins supple.

When on the horse, we must be at rest and not agitate ourselves. On the horse, we must be "a rider" and not "a passenger" shaken by every jerk of movement.

We must feel the horse with our buttocks, in particular, we must feel on which leg the horse departs at the canter, true or counter-canter, and not ride a horse like a bicycle with insensitive buttocks.

Be careful that the branches [shanks] of the curb are symmetrical in relation to the mouth.

A horse that has a "mute mouth"[37] is not a light horse.

Divisions of contacts: [for instance, hold] the left snaffle rein in the left hand and the right curb rein in the right hand[38].

"The fixed hand" is the hand that contracts itself to vanquish a resistance and then releases while remaining immobile. Therefore, there is no movement of the hand, only the fingers that act.

If your horse resists on the left side, try to replace [the action] of the left rein by the aid of the left leg.

The heels must be neither too high, nor too low: it is ugly [these excessive positions of the lower leg]and indicates a contraction of the ankles.

Important rule: independence of the legs. When we act with one leg, we must manage to be sure that the other one doesn't glue itself to the horse nor move; in short [each leg] must remain independent from what the other leg does.

Comparison: the forehand and the hind-end of the horse are the two sides of the scale and the riders' torso is the fulcrum. The rider can therefore, put weight at will on either end of the horse.

Comment on the fixed hand: to fix the hand is the same as the horse having two side reins. To fix the hand, we must push [the horse forward with the buttocks] and close the fingers without the hand moving a millimeter backwards. The [fixed] hand cannot follow the horse's head [movements]. If need be, it must oppose itself [to any attempt of evasion by the horse]. The hand cannot be moved out of place by the horse's mouth. The horse must come [slightly] behind the hand [but cannot go behind the legs] and he cannot go beyond the hand [either with his head].

In fact, it is not a rein issue, it's a leg issue. The legs act and the hand does not, the hand fixes itself to place the horse [in the *ramener* position].

If there is resistance, the hand should not give. It resists in the resistance and it gives in the release. Never the contrary or the horse will not understand.

_____ In short, it is push, take [hold] and give.

37   [a mouth without any activity]
38   [Usually hold the curb in the outside rein of the turn or the circle and hold the bridoon on the inside of the of the turn or circle]

The rider and the horse must form a single body: *the centaur.*

Some absolute necessities:
1. It is necessary to be one with the horse, particularly by sitting in a good position.
2. It is necessary to not have any weight on the reins [when the horse is round].
3. It is necessary to have quick, lightning-like reflexes.

Examples for the hands: if the horse forces [the hand], the fingers should tighten immediately and release as soon as he releases.

Examples for the legs: if the horse brings the croup away from the wall, intervene immediately with the inside leg.

Master Oliveira also says: "If the horse brings the croup away from the wall, place the shoulders in front of the haunches and then push the horse back to the wall with lateral aids."

"I am not interested in seeing riders who move. *You must work through your thoughts.*"

If the horse is bent too much, he loses his impulsion and his cadence. With a horse that bends too much use the outside lateral aids. For instance, if a horse bends too much to the left, use the right hand and leg.

To be *"one with the horse"* it is not only just to sit, but also to sit in such a way that we don't lose contact with the saddle if the horse spooks. We must remain sitting to be able to keep the horse in place.

To achieve this goal, the reins must not be abandoned. Therefore, the horse must be in "the channel of the aids" (with a fixed hand).

The fixed, immobile hand: the elbows close to the body must not move backwards. The fingers become fixed (quivering or convulsive fingers, as Beudant used to say), but the hand should not come backwards even one centimeter. If a stronger tension is needed, it is the waist that leans backwards. After the horse releases, the waist comes forward towards the pommel of the saddle and the fingers relax but the hand has not moved [on its own].

The hand is a filter. We must know what quantity [of energy] we must let through in relation to the exercise we are attempting.

The horse and the rider must be in one piece. The hands must accompany and not oppose the movement.

The hands must not be static. No part of the body must be static either and everything must be constantly readjusted. Regarding the hands, when they have been properly placed they must not be static [dead] but to the contrary, they must act discretely in a restricted space. In the small circular space [in front of the waist], searching for – in each moment – the position of the hand that the horse accepts most willingly.

Be economical with your aids. If you use too much leg, you will have to hold the horse back more. This excess results in a lack of delicacy and pointless waste.

Not everyone can be elegant on a horse, but everyone can be correct on a horse. Stiff elegance is the aspect of riding that is most destructive to forward movement. What matters is correctness.

In the execution of an exercise, the intensity of the aid must vary as a function of the horse's response to the demand.

Whatever the position of the reins are [inside or outside] they must have, more or less, the same intensity of contact. An important point about circles is that the contact must be the same on both reins.

When the reins float, there can be two reasons:

1. Lack of impulsion of the horse.
2. A lack of fixity of the rider in the saddle.

The use of side reins with rubber rings create the habit of the horse swinging the head up and down. When the horse pulls, the rings give; the horse gives, the rings pull. It's ridiculous. Because when he feels that he wins by pulling, it gives him the opportunity to bob the head.

Equitation is the art of staying quiet on a horse.

If you do a lengthening of the walk by using the spurs, you lose all feelings of cadence.

If your hands move, it is because your waist is not relaxed. I want an immobile hand with mobile fingers. And when I say "fix your hands" it means close the fingers convulsively without the hands moving backwards.

Give the impression that everything you do is easy.

Prepare the exercise, because every action should not be a surprise.

Fixing the hand is not pulling: it is immobilizing it. To vanquish a resistance you close the hand. When the horse releases you open it to reward while keeping the contact and this must be done for the life of the horse. If you have the hand fixed all the time, the horse becomes nervous or dead to the aids. It is necessary to resist in the precise moment and release in the precise moment.

Adjusting your reins: if they are too long: you risk losing the contact. If they are too short: you risk either jerkiness or blocking the horse.

Act little but in the exact moment: Use delicate gestures that do not surprise the horse. [In order to address the whole of the horse,] you must precede the action of the hand with the adjustment of the torso; otherwise you are only attached to the head of the horse.

The shoulders of the rider are back while the waist is forward [at the same time], but we do not bring the shoulders back on their own [without the waist going forward, because if the back AND the loins AND the seat go back together,] we are going against the movement [and blocking the oscillations of the horse's back].

If I say "take more contact," it doesn't mean pull. It is adjusting the reins a little more and maintaining the constancy of the contact.

The hands follow the haunches of the horse through the link of your waist that advances [with each stride] and follows the movements of the horse.

Try to obtain all of the movement without effort, meaning without employing the aids too strongly, but with the same vibration [energy and cadence] of the gait.

The wrists of the rider must never be rigid. Instead, they must be relaxed and immobile without stiffness, ready to influence [the mouth]. Bend the wrist slightly as if you were holding two candles.

Don't always use the aids with the same intensity. Use the intensity of aids that corresponds to the horse that has responded with a release [of the mouth and back].

We release if he has released.

We must not confuse "pulling" and "fixing." To fix the hand the reins must be adjusted.

The shoulders of the rider must be parallel to the shoulders of the horse unless we want to oppose a resistance for a moment[39].

The torso of the rider can only act effectively if the reins are at a good length.

Try to obtain everything with light aids.

The principle aid of the rider is the torso. It is the fundamental piece: the waist and the torso. Therefore, we must [maintain] a correct position. Compare [the action of the torso] with the fulcrum of the scale. Only after [the torso's action] comes the use of the hands and legs.

The principle aid: the torso. And it is by luck that the rider also has arms and legs.

The body of the rider must move with the movement of the horse, except if it must momentarily oppose it.

With all horses, it is sufficient to use a very small action of the waist to dominate the horse.

---

39   [Bring one shoulder back to oppose the resistance]

The correct position is the one that bothers the horse the least and allows us to use the aids the most effectively.

In principle, the torso of the rider rests immobile, but may intervene like the fulcrum of the scale to rectify [a loss of balance] as if the forehand and the back end of the horse were the two trays of the scale.

The torso can have a great influence on the equilibrium of the horse. It can push, support or slow down.

The back of the rider has more importance than the reins. What we need is not a rigid back ("don't swallow an umbrella"), but a relaxed torso with loins that move[40] [to the movement desired].

The neck of the rider must not be rigid.

If your arms do not rest on your hips, it is not your torso that acts, but your arms that act. Therefore, keep your elbows to the body.

It is the largest part of the foot that must rest of the stirrup, meaning the part just behind the toes [the ball of the foot]. The foot rests on the stirrup, but don't push on the stirrups, otherwise the entire leg is contracted.

I do not like the spurs placed high on the ankle. It creates a risk of touching the horse without being aware of it. The spurs placed low permit us to do more delicate touches by lifting the heel (even if it's less aesthetic). In principle the heel stays in place, but it can be mobile by lifting to bring the spur into action and then return to its normal position.

It is necessary for the body of the rider to always be accorded with the direction of the movement of the horse. It must not oppose it[41].

Don't block the horse with your hands (hold and give).

Relax your wrists.

Releasing is not abandoning, it is ceasing the action.

It is easy to release, what is difficult is to hold again after a release.

Nuno Oliveira shows to a rider how to take [the contact] again after a release by using the torso by arching the back and fixating it for an instant: "take with your waist."

We take to vanquish a resistance, we release to reward.

Take means to close [*serrer*] the fingers.

Release means to open [*desserrer*] the fingers.

In academic equitation, we must move the arms as little as possible and the fingers as much as possible. Closing and opening the fingers with a hand that never moves back.

To young riders:

---

40   *joue*
41   [except when resistances are present]

1. It is not by the spur that we obtain impulsion, it is by the action of the buttocks and your waist.

2. Don't compress your horses, let them execute all of these exercises in forward motion.

3. If you are yourself contracted, you will transmit your contraction to the movement of the horse.

Rule: do not stay attached to the mouth of the horse.

The spur is a reinforcement of the leg. Therefore, only utilize it when the leg is not sufficient, and as little as possible with good timing and wisely. The spur must touch the horse from a relaxed leg.

What does it mean to adjust the aids?

1. It means to have the legs close so as not to surprise the horse if they must intervene.

2. Hold the reins in such a way that you do not need to advance or bring back the arms in order to adjust [the reins].

A rule:

1. Avoid releasing during the moment when the horse resists.

2. But the other danger is to not releasing at the moment when the horse releases.

If the horse rips the reins out of your hands in order to stretch his neck, you must resist because it is a resistance. The neck stretch is good, but only when requested [by the rider].

Equitation is more feeling than thinking.

Act little, but with good timing.

The rider's reflex when the horse goes too fast is to pull on the reins. This is a mistake. There are other means to use: the torso, the circle, etc.

To practice good equitation, we need:

1. A bit of the waist.

2. A bit of the head.

3. And also, a bit of the heart.

The rider often does too much. If he is quiet, the horse is also quiet. In order to be able to follow [the horse's] mouth by the waist [of the rider], (and this is what must be done), we need the reins to be adjusted in order to establish the contact.

Before giving *a little jerk*[42], we must let go of the reins a little bit and not do it on a tight rein.

The horse has more strength than the rider, therefore, the rider must use his intelligence against the horse's strength. For example, by choosing the most appropriate moment for transitions, etc.

[Nuno Oliveira said] to a beginner: if the rider's feet creep forward, the waist cannot function properly.

In an exercise (a half-pass for instance) if a horse rushes, it is because he is resisting.

If the action of the hand is necessary, it must be done upwards and never from front to back.

In the trot, neither the hand nor the ankle must "trot." Because when they move, they create contraction and the torso cannot feel what is happening in the horse's back and you will transmit your stiffness to the horse. Therefore, you must have relaxed legs and ankles in the trot. If needed, if it is necessary to wake up the horse, intervene quickly and then leave him alone.

A horse who is working through the use of force can perform movements and figures, but it will be in rigidity and to the detriment of lightness; [working in force] is always to the detriment of the horse's physique and morale.

The horse in hand[43]: Academic equitation starts with the *horse in hand.* It is not the rider that must create this situation by pulling, but it is the horse who must seek the connection with the hand. The forehead must be vertical and the horse light.

The horse in hand is *placed* [in *ramener*], rounded, in impulsion and in self carriage. You only need to adjust the reins as the mouth is already relaxed.

The horse takes the connection himself. He grows from the front, elevating and positions[44] himself. Then he becomes light.

`He has engaged his hind legs, rounded his walk and established a contact with the hand, more or less light according to his sensitivity.

The *horse in hand*[45] adopts the position in which he feels the most at ease and in which he gives his back without becoming heavy, yet keeps the contact [connection].

At the canter, the horse in hand is the one which keeps the same

---

42   *une petit saccade* [A little jerk on the mouth is one of the ways Nuno used to dissipate a resistance.]
43   *mise en main*
44   *se place*
45   *mise en main*

position of the head, the same cadence, the same speed, the same degree of energy and the same degree of contact.

The horse in hand:
1. The hand must always be in communication with the mouth.
2. But it must be the horse, at the request of the rider's legs, that takes the contact himself. The hand should not come backward to find the mouth. The horse that pulls is not "on the hand": he is beyond the hand. Hence, the necessity of the lightness of contact.

Speak to your horse; the voice is an important aid.

Having a light hand doesn't mean to abandon the horse [losing the contact with loose reins]. It is also not blocking the horse with the hand [holding him too tight constantly]. It is maintaining the reins adjusted and pushing [the horse forward with the waist]. "Hold and give" so the horse doesn't lean [on the hand].

The contact is not getting hold of the horse's head [by force], but it is the light contact the horse takes because he is being sent onto the hand[46].

[Riding on a] completely loose rein (which has been called the "poetry of equitation"), guiding the horse on the "weight of the reins," while he is behind the hand but in front of the legs, is only doable with a horse [perfectly] trained and ridden by an exceptional rider, at the condition that the horse remains perfectly light and maintains his position. Otherwise it is "abandonment"[47]. Therefore, as this summit [of the art] is rarely attained, we need a contact[48], but a soft contact, without weight, not with a horse that falls asleep on the hand.

Between weightiness and the [correct] contact, there is a world of difference. This is why [we must find] the right measure, the "dose."

We can bring the torso momentarily backwards to sit the horse more [on his haunches]. But if we do it all the time, we oppose the forward movement [by overloading the haunches].

Fundamental training principle: prepare and let it be. The result of this principle is the quality of the transitions between gaits.

The more advanced a horse's training, the less we need to insist on the aids. For instance, after two or three correct steps of shoulder-in, we must reduce or even completely cease the aids. The horse has released, so the rider needs to release as well, otherwise the horse doesn't understand.

Role of the inside leg at the canter: it is the inside leg that pushes

46   [by the forward action of the waist]
47   [loss of connection]
48   [to maintain the connection]

54

[the horse forward], [but we must remember] that the inside leg is a wall that the horse must never force. This is particularly important with the Iberian horses who have a high degree of lateral mobility; but it is an elastic wall, not one made of concrete. This comment on the inside leg is particularly important when we start the flying changes.

The inside leg also supports the inside rein to obtain and maintain the inside bend.

If we give a touch with the whip to activate the horse, it must be done with the reins adjusted.

The rider's back cannot function correctly if the legs are contracted. If you glue the legs to the horse's sides, you will stiffen the rest of your body and you communicate this rigidity to the horse. Besides, your legs will not be in a position that allows them to act quickly. The rider's legs should be not glued to the horse, but attentive [close by and ready to act]. If you tighten the knees (except in the case of a spook), the action of the leg is limited and will prevent you from using it normally[49].

The continual back and forth movement of the rider's feet is like the tick-tock of the clock after a good lunch: it puts the horse to sleep.

Fingers that close and that open to reward, with an immobile hand, is more effective than a hand that moves.

Don't carry your horse with your spurs all the time, as it will render him dull and take away his spirit.

It is the rider's shoulders that determine the direction [of the horse], and not the actions of the hand.

Always control the cadence: it is useful to close your eyes for three strides because it helps concentration.

When we lose the contact [connection], we lose the control of the horse and he begins to be in charge.

In the lateral work, one leg orders and the other one receives[50].

Descente de mains, descente de jambes (yielding of the hands and legs) does not necessarily mean to open the hands and spread the legs, it means to cease their action.

The touch of the spur and the whip [to increase the energy of the horse]. The touch must be delicate and electric. The leg must not press nor glue itself [to the horse's sides], it must do an [instantaneous] on and off.

The touch must be sharp, like the plucking of a guitar string.

Legs without bones [no tension in the articulation of the knee or the ankle].

49   [It must be added that Oliveira never tightened his thighs or his knees but frequently applied the lower leg while using the stirrup as a point of leverage to use either the calf, ankle or the spur]

50   [the lateral displacement]

The touch of the spur is done with a soft leg that is relaxed. In the same way, the touch of the whip must be electric and not rest on the horse.

The use of force, if need be, is something that must happen in a fraction of a second, not longer.

If the rider moves the leg too much, he or she will not have the possibility of receiving the sensations [from the horse's body]. Such a leg is not "listening" to the horse.

Any system [of auxiliary rein or tack] (such as the Chambon, the draw reins, the curb with a big tongue liberty) must be used temporarily to correct a problem; then we return to the normal [equipment]. What can be used routinely, is lunging with side reins[51].

Tightening the curb chain to fight weight resistances, is a negative short cut. It resolves problems only temporarily and will escalate the need for more and more[52].

The intensity of the aids to be used depends on the horse ridden, of his finesse [degree of response to the aids], his sensitivity and his nervous energy.

Hold and release: when we need to close the fingers, we must also push the waist forward[53].

To go through corners [properly], the role of the inside rein must be replaced by the action of the inside leg.

The leg of impulsion: in the shoulder-in it is the outside leg; in the half-pass, it is the inside leg.

A dressage rider must ride with the hands close to the navel, and not with the arms stretched forward.

Normally - except in the case of a momentary opposition [to the horse's resistance] – the rider's shoulders must remain parallel to the horse's shoulders.

The hands must act from lower to higher. It is the gesture of the hand bringing a soup spoon to the mouth. If we act from front to back, we are always occupied with fighting.

Absolute rule: release when the horse releases.

The majority of the riders use full force with horses that pull, use partial force with horses that pull a little, and abandon [the contact] with horses with no energy. This is not what horsemanship is about.

51   [Nuno Oliveira routinely used side reins with check reins adjusted a little long to prevent the horse from lowering his head too much when lunged. This combination side reins/check reins is also called the Hanoverian rein]

52   [A short curb chain tends to pinch tongue and lips and is painful to the horse]

53   [to push the horse on the bit]

With the aids, be economical. Don't do supplementary things beyond what is necessary.

It is fundamentally important to be *quick with the actions* of the hand, legs, the "plucking" of the spur used with a soft, relaxed leg. Never use continuous aids.

Holding [fixing the hand] is not pulling; it is adjusting the reins at such a length that the horse will take the contact at the desired moment.

Caressing the horse is a good thing but at the precise moment [it is needed], and not all the time. If the horse is worried, we calm him by caresses and by the voice. But if he is not worried, it is by energetic work that we calm him.

The quality of gait we are in determines the quality of the gait we will transition into.

Training the horse is a continuous series of transitions from *"l'effet d'ensemble"* [comprehensive effect] to the *descente de main et de jambes* [yielding of the aids], which means to stop acting. In other words, hold and release. When I say release, I mean: "open the fingers without losing the contact" [and relax the legs].

Many riders let their horses weigh 60 pounds on their hands during an hour without result. It is better to oppose the forces to 120 pounds for a fraction of a second [and get a release]. That is effective.

If we pull on the horse's mouth, no lightness is possible.

Between the *vibration* (rustling of the wrist) and the jerk[54], there is an entire range.[55]

The majority of riders have legs that are too slow [to act]. To be able to use them quickly, the legs must be completely relaxed. "Legs without bones" [no tension in the knee and ankle].

The fixed hand[56] is a hand that doesn't move [in relation to the horse's back]. It requires a relaxed waist. Only the fingers move (fingers of a pianist).

Rule: never make nervous gestures on a horse, stay calm and maintain your self control.

We must respect the right dose of aids, because if we push too much, the horse becomes rigid.

To be "one with the horse" consists of following the back of the horse with our own back.

Baucher used to say: the abuse of diagonal effects puts the horse

---

54 *saccade*

55 [of actions to choose from when we need to act on the horse's mouth to re-establish lightness]

56 *main fixe*

in rigidity[57]. The ideal is to put the horse in a diagonal position by using lateral effects[58].

Use slow and soft movements but have rapid reflexes.

Nuno Oliveira says to a rider: "we do not ride with the hands on the withers [except for beginners, as advised elsewhere]. The hand must be in front of the navel."

Try to obtain results with a minimum of aids, but without letting the horse sleep. In this case [the horse might "fall asleep," lose energy] use a little touch [of the leg or the whip].

When the rider is sitting poorly (lack of basic seat), he or she will pull on the reins and become attached to the mouth of the horse.

Riding a sequence of exercises consists of preparing each exercise [appropriately] and never surprising the horse.

To relax the horse, the aids must be delicate. Do not surprise the horse with the legs.

When you perform an exercise, try to finish it with the aids in position of demand [hands and legs], but without action. Therefore, do not end the exercise with the same intensity of aids with which you started it.

In principle the body of the rider must move very little, but it so happens that with young horses, a little movement helps.

Use of the long [dressage] *whip*: widen the position of the hand that holds the whip and also widen the other one to keep the horse straight. Touch the croup at mid-height [by swiveling the wrist on its axis].

Do not grab the reins, because it blocks the horse. If needed, play with your fingertips.

It is necessary to observe the head of the horse (poll, ears), but we must pay attention that the base of the neck doesn't get crooked, which generally happens when the rider uses too much inside rein.

If the hands of the riders are static, the horse will have a tendency to lean on the reins.

The role of the *spur attacks*[59] is to collect the horse. It does not mean to employ force. This process of the "attacks" is necessary as it belongs to the education of the horse. But these attacks must be performed with a light hand, and the attacks should also be light (like little bee stings)

57   [A diagonal effect consists of using one hand to control one shoulder and the opposite leg to engage the horse. This diagonal effect is used to create a diagonal action in the horse and to collect him, for instance in the preparation of piaffe]

58   [Lateral effects consist of using the hand and leg of the same side. I am guessing that Nuno Oliveira means to use both lateral effects in succession to get the horse collected]

59   *attacques d'éperon*

58

and also very quick (performed with a relaxed leg).

A horse that doesn't admit the lesson of the "attacks" without staying round as a ball and light in hand, without complaining and resisting is not a trained horse.

A trained horse must also know *l'effet d'ensemble* [comprehensive effect].

Don't lose sight of this fundamental *"sésame"*[60]: go from one concept to the other fluidly.[61]

People say: "push the horse on the hand." It is a mistake. It is not the rider that imposes the contact, it is the horse who establishes a soft contact because of the use of appropriate exercises.

With a young horse, we use the hand to give direction (opening rein), but as training progresses, we economize the hands in order to give direction by the legs [and the seat and shoulders].

What matters is to find the exact dose that is appropriate at each moment for each exercise.

Three concepts will "place" a horse:[62]
1. Quiet hands
2. Aids that do not surprise
3. [Maintaining] the cadence

For a horse that has a tendency to place his head and his croup to the right, he will not be straightened out by the action of the right rein nor of the right leg. Instead, use the left rein to replace the shoulders in front of the quarters and [line him up] with the wall. With such a horse, it is useful to finish the lesson with exercises that send the haunches to the left (like right shoulder-in or left half-pass, etc.).

Concerning the rule: *"push, hold, and release,"* it doesn't mean:
1. Push --- hold --- release [with a delay between each phase]
It is push/hold/release instantaneously, in a fraction of a second.

We must release in a timely manner. If it lasts more than a fraction of second, it becomes force.

2. And at the moment we release, we must feel in what measure. If we release too little, the horse will get excited, and resist. If we release too much, it puts the horse on the forehand.

---

60   *sésame* [Concept that opens all doors by magic.]
61   [As mentioned here: roundness and activity by the attacks, roundness and complete calm by *l'effet d'ensemble*]
62   *placer* [achieve the complete *ramener* or vertical position of the forehead with a light contact and a raised base of the neck]

I repeat: in the exercise, we must manage to keep the reins in position, but without action. This is the ideal we must seek.

Release is not abandoning [the contact], it is ceasing to act.

We must go from one movement to the next quickly, but without roughness and without hitches.

Many riders seem to ignore that the horse has a jaw. They practice an equitation of concrete.

Work with the draw reins (sliding): we must resist when the horse resists and release *as soon as* he releases. Otherwise he won't understand. [Nuno Oliveira used draw reins occasionally with horses with difficult necks, but he never used them to over-flex the horses].

If we have the spurs glued to the sides all the time, how do you expect the horse to understand the action of the spur?

In the lateral work, it is important that the horse moves because of the exercise itself and not by the reins. There must be no weight in either rein.

Before taking a diagonal [to change rein] at the canter for example, we must start looking at the diagonal line when we are riding on the short side, in order to see how we are going to take it [prepare the geometry of the diagonal].

If the wrist is not supple, the hand cannot function normally even if the hand is not rigid itself.

The [average] rider uses his or her hands. "*L'écuyer*"[63] uses his legs [and torso and seat].

We do not turn on the diagonal or on the center line by the inside rein that holds back, but by the outside rein [that allows and contains].

The role of the outside rein in canter can be helped by the outside shoulder that comes back a little.

If we bring the legs back too much, we contract the horse's haunches.

We negotiate a loop [in a serpentine for instance] by advancing the outside shoulder and acting with the inside leg close to the girth to support the horse [preventing him from falling on the inside shoulder].

The rider must respect a number of small details, such as the length of the reins etc.. If for example, the reins are too long, the elbows cannot function with the torso. They must be in one piece with the torso [to be effective and for the reins to transmit every movement of the torso, the central aid of the educated rider]. Too long a rein prevent the rein to follow the action of the torso.

To a rider: "if you hold your hands above the withers, you are lean-

---

63   [the master trainer]

ing forward and your position doesn't allow you to hold and release, nor support the horse with your torso."

We cannot collect a horse if the torso of the rider is not vertical. In this case we hang on the reins.

As the horse progresses, you replace the hands by the legs to give direction. For the average rider, the legs are only used to push the horse forward. For the true trainer, the legs are used to
1) frame the horse [in the channel of the aids],
2) bend the horse,
3) give direction,
4) relax the jaw [by *l'effet d'ensemble*] and
5) halt [engage the horse in the transition down].

Riding a horse [correctly] consists in being one with the horse[64] and do very little things [use discreet, relaxed aids].

Remember: the rein on the side where the horse has a natural bend [turns his head] must be a little lighter than the other.

The legs must always precede the action of the hands.

Remember: when the fingers open, they must not lose the contact. To give is not the abandonment of the reins, it is to cease to act.

When a horse has a bend more difficult than the other, we must not pull on the rein on this side but rather use the leg on this same side. In doing so, replace the rein by the leg.

Don't be attached to the horse's mouth, without abandoning [losing contact].

A fixed hand is a hand that doesn't take hold of the horse's mouth but is not taken by the horse's mouth either. Fixing allows the hand, if need be, to contract convulsively for one second. Fixing means resist in the precise moment and then release [quickly].

The rider's legs must be attentive, so they must stay close to the horse but relaxed.

In Latin Equitation [dressage of the French Tradition]: the legs precede the hand and the hand is a barrier that the horse cannot go beyond. Once this demand is respected by the horse, the hand releases.

If, in an exercise, we need to intervene with one particular leg, the other one must stay in place.

For flying changes for instance, the other leg (the one that doesn't intervene) cannot go forward. This means that the rider must maintain independent legs, each in relation to the other.

"All pretexts are good to practice the *descente de main* [yielding of the hand].

---

64   [through the suppleness of the loins]

When we are teaching the *effet d'ensemble*, the depart from the halt is done with a light pressure of the spur. When the horse is well-trained to it, the depart is done by opening the legs [*descente de jambs*, yielding of the legs].

I repeat that when we *doubler* [crossing the arena either by going parallel to the short side – *doubler* in the width of the arena – or by going parallel to the long side – *doubler* in the length of the arena], or when we turn short, we must not neglect the role of the inside leg so the horse doesn't fall on the inside shoulder, otherwise the cadence will be altered.

The advice that I give most often in [my clinics] around the world is "have light hands."

When the hand is not fixed, the young horse becomes accustomed to moving his head all the time.

The more a horse advances in his training, the more we use the legs for direction instead of the hands. With a trained horse, the hand is only used to:

1) Maintain the head in the correct position and

2) Control the speed.

Double bridle: if we put two pieces in the horse's mouth (bridoon and curb), it is not to use them both together with the same degree of pressure in a constant manner.

Usefulness of working with the reins in one hand (the curb reins adjusted in the left hand, the snaffle reins completely loose on the outside [of the curb reins]):

1) It refines the aids and teaches [the rider] to control the horse with the legs.

2) It permits to verify the straightness and the collection

3) It shows us if the horse is truly in the "corridor of the aids"

What is a truly soft contact? It is a contact that doesn't get hold of the horse's mouth by force but doesn't abandon it either.

The good hand is the one that doesn't get hold of the mouth by force but is not controlled by the horse's mouth either.

The fixed hand must prevent the horse from rushing.

When we work a horse "in-hand," the horse follows your steps. We must therefore walk "in step" with the horse, in rhythm with him. This prevents jerkiness.

When during work "in-hand," we leave the wall and take the diagonal, this is done by the handler stepping backward and placing himself or herself slightly in front of the horse rather than on his side.

The harder the use of the spur, the more the horse becomes rigid. Therefore use the spur delicately and appropriately.

If, when you turn the head of the horse in a certain direction, the rein on that side is lighter, you will find that this will greatly facilitate many aspects of the horse's education.

Before initiating any exercise, verify the impulsion and then let the horse act. Just watch over the execution.

The reins must be used to maintain the rhythm and control the position of the head, nothing more.

If the legs of the rider move constantly, the horse loses his sensitivity and the rider too!

To say, "put your shoulders back" is not a good expression, because the rider can do it and maintain nevertheless a rigid waist. It is better to say: "lower the waist and push your navel forward toward your hands." It is no longer the hands that move towards the navel, but the inverse.

We must not work the resisting side so much more, but rather pay more attention to the aids on that side.

If the rider doesn't release when the horse releases, this is what provokes the apparition of weight resistances.

"Moving the contact" consists of advancing the hands a little so the horse lengthens his neck by a few inches.

When the horse has yielded in a session of lateral work, I advise you to go on the straight [to maintain the impulsion].

Never lose sight of the proportion to be used between the actions of the hands and the actions of the legs.

During the warm-up work, it is a good idea to have less tension in the reins than in the work that follows.

In principle the rider's shoulders should parallel the horse's shoulders; when we begin a corner, the rider must advance the outside shoulder.

When we do canter on a circle, we must not put weight on the outside stirrup, instead, always load a little bit on the inside stirrup.

What matters, is not our elegance [in the saddle], but it is [to adopt] the most effective position for using the aids.

Function of the hands: to control the position [of the head and neck], and the speed. Function of the legs to: give impulsion, collect, direct, calm.

The rider must maintain [the energy] of the hind-end and then receive in his hand the contact with the mouth. Therefore, the rider must not shorten the reins and advance the hands, because that would be "taking"[65] the horse.

In civilized equitation, we place the horse by the legs. In rudimen-

---

65   *"prendre"*

tary equitation, one places the horse by the action of the hands. In civilized equitation, to correct matters (if the horse becomes tense) we return to the walk, [to resolve the problem through exercises of relaxation]. In rudimentary equitation, riders push, pull, prod, extend.

Hands without legs, legs without hands [important principle of Baucher], *when the legs are acting*, the hands doesn't oppose their action, but they are there. Not "nonexistent" hands, up-in-the-air.
When the hands are acting, the legs are not open, they are without action, but they supervise.

This principle [of Hands without Legs and Legs without Hands] is to be used with the young horses. On the contrary, in the *effet d'ensemble*, there are two forces that oppose each other. This must be used with trained horses.

More comments on the fixed hand:
To "fix" can be compared with the use of side reins.

To fix the hand, we must push [with the waist] and close the fingers but without the hand moving one millimeter backwards. However the hands must not follow the horse's head either. If needed, the hand must oppose [any force the horse might use]. The hands cannot be taken by the horse's mouth. The horse comes behind the hand [by a very small amount] and cannot go beyond.

In fact it is not a question of reins, it is a question of legs. The legs act, the hand doesn't. Instead the hands are fixed to place the horse [position the head and neck]. It is an action of legs without action of hand. If there is resistance, the hand cannot release. It resists in the resistance, it releases in the release, not the opposite. Otherwise the horse will not understand. In short, it is push -- hold and release. The horse and the rider form only one body: it is the centaur.

Chapter 3

IMPULSION, CADENCE, LIGHTNESS, BALANCE

Cadence and impulsion.

"Each horse achieves cadence not by the hand of the rider but by the appropriate exercise which prepares him. I would like Antoine [de Coux, the author of this book] to make this important note."
-Nuno Oliveira

To have cadence is to have a metronome in our head.

Without cadence, there is no equitation of value.

If a horse succeeds at an exercise without cadence, it is only by luck and it is never perfectly successful.

The beauty of dressage work is in maintaining the same cadence.

In the trot, you don't need to push with the legs or slow down with the hands, if you have a correct cadence.

Generally, riders know that to do an upward transition, from walk to trot for example, they need to create a walk with more impulsion by increasing the cadence of the walk. What they understand less readily is that it is also by an increase of impulsion and not by abandoning the reins that they will achieve a downward transition.

Speed and impulsion have nothing to do with each other.[66] There is no cadence without impulsion and no impulsion without cadence.

The more impulsion a horse has, the more forward he is, the easier it is to keep him straight.

When your horse loses the contact and moves his head, push, because he is losing impulsion.

To increase the impulsion in the walk does not consist of getting a more rapid walk but a more energetic walk[67].

When a horse is capable of keeping the cadence in the walk and staying in the hand, many problems are resolved.

In an extension, do not pass the point where you are able to control [the horse].

In the transitions, pay attention to the fixity of the head. For if the horse swings the head, it is because he no longer engages the hind legs

66   [We need to determine and control both of them in a way that suits each individual horse]

67   [more movement and elevation but with less speed]

and there is a lack of impulsion. The cornerstone of impulsion is the fixity of the head during the transitions.

Extensions.

After an extension, we must "take control" delicately again in order not to hollow the horse and make him rigid, otherwise we will damage the work done previously.

Contrary to what many riders do, we must not let the horse get on the forehand in an extension. The horse must stay collected in the extension.[68]

To judge the quality of an extension, we must look at the hind legs as much as the front legs. The hind legs must push.

In an extension, we must be satisfied with what the horse can offer. It is better for the extension to have less speed and keep his cadence, rather than achieve more speed and rush.

Think about the degree of energy required before the extension, sufficient but not excessive, in order to maintain control. Prepare and execute the second corner [of the short side] as well as possible. Stabilize [the neck] for the first two strides of the diagonal, then let the neck stretch out a little without losing the contact.[69] It is only in the "high level tests" [Grand Prix and Grand Prix Special] that the horse must extend with the neck in a high position.

Then think about the way to slow down the horse at the end of the diagonal, in suppleness and without force. If force is necessary, the horse will stiffen his back and we risk losing the benefit of the work done.

It is on the center line that we verify if the horse is straight. The control of the horse's straightness can be done on the long side, but it is relative. It is better to control it by taking the center line in cadence.

The horse in walk, in trot, must be straight, not just appear straight, but also feel straight to the rider. What does this mean? It is when the rider is sitting in the axis of the horse comfortably and the horse doesn't push [the rider] neither to the left nor the right.

Two different manners of straightening the horse:

1) If the horse becomes crooked involuntarily, replace the shoulders in front of the haunches.

2) If the horse resists actively (the horse being on the left rein):

---

68   [This means, following the advice of Nuno Oliveira , that we must control the position of the forehand, keep it elevated]

69   [Young horses can stretch the neck further and the more advanced they become, the less they need to do it]

66

ask the horse to half-pass to the right to the wall.[70]

Dressage consists in developing movements that are both slow and energetic.

The equitation of dressage begins by the positioning of the head, by the fixity of the poll, and by the "horse in the hand."

Impulsion has nothing to do with the speed. Impulsion begins by the mind of the horse, not by his legs.

To increase impulsion, increasing the speed is a false but easy solution. What is needed is to increase the energy without increasing speed.[71]

The beauty of all the work at the walk, trot, is that it must happen in the same rhythm, the same cadence.

The *cadence* is something very important, more important than many people think.

The cadence is rhythm [tempo] with energy.

The maintenance of the cadence is the beauty of dressage.

To push does not mean increasing the gait by increasing the speed.[72]

Lightness is the fruit of impulsion.[73]

The sequence of exercises creates impulsion because the horse is obliged to be attentive and to work.

Before starting an exercise, what is needed? Impulsion.

To resolve a problem, what is needed? Impulsion. [Nuno Oliveira used to call impulsion "the aspirin of equitation"].

Prepare [the horse] by adopting the position and the [degree] of impulsion necessary for the chosen exercise. Before the exercise, verify if [the horse] is truly forward, in front of the legs and stable in his position.

It is pointless to begin the exercise if the horse's head is up in the air [above the bit] and if he is "floating."

Advice to a beginning rider: "Right now, you need to forget [all of these advanced preoccupations], forget about a fancy warm up, forget

---

70   [Straighten the horse by a firm action of the leg to deviate the haunches-in a direction opposite to the one they want to adopt]

71   [At the very beginning of training, increasing the speed helps create impulsion when the horse doesn't have any collection yet (see the chapter on the work on young horses where Nuno Oliveira insists that they are worked only in medium gaits with hardly any contact). Increasing energy without increasing speed comes after the horse has developed a good connection and a correct position of the forehand ("*ramené*")]

72   [Nuno Oliveira means pushing with the waist moving toward the hands at every stride. Pushing is the action that increases the energy of the stride].

73   [This is very important in Nuno Oliveira's thinking, because he hated the false lightness achieved by "abandoning" the contact].

about lightness, forget about everything. For you right now: "go forward and jump some fences."

In the entire work, it is important that the rider get the feeling that the haunches are pushing the body of the horse, not that they are following it.

We must not confuse lightness with false lightness, in which a rider, under the pretext of lightness, let his horse float without impulsion.

Relaxation [*decontraction*] is not lack of energy.

The tact: feeling in advance if the horse is about to lose his impulsion. Afterwards, it's too late.

The contact [connection]: to make the horse "come up on the hand" is feeling that the poll flexes, the back lifts and the hind legs engage.

It is by creating a sequence of exercises, passing [fluidly] from one to the other, so that the horse becomes supple. Therefore, do not stay in the same exercise for very long. The sequence creates straightness with flexibility.

True straightness consists of being able, while riding on the center line, to perform at any moment, a correct circle in either direction.

If you can, in all three gaits, ride the center line really straight and perform a 6 meter circle to either side [with the same degree of lightness of the aids]. Then your horse is really trained.

The cadence is the rhythm [tempo] more collected, more controlled. The beauty of dressage work is the maintenance of a constant cadence.

The horse becomes obligated to use himself more when asked to perform accurate figures.

When you lose the control of the cadence, the horse starts to take control (because he becomes "open")[74]. When the rider controls the cadence, it is he that is in command.

In the transitions between gaits, the poll must remain at the same height. This is a basic principle.

Resistances disappear when the weight is [sufficiently] on the haunches.

[Academic] Equitation is when a horse remains "vibrant" [full of contained energy] on light reins.

Impulsion has nothing to do with speed. It is the vibration of the energy. When I say "push," I don't mean "go faster," I mean "increase the vibration."

---

74   [Open is the opposite of collected, It means strung out, disengaged and above the bit to any degree]

Each horse enters into cadence not by the hand of the rider, but by the appropriate exercise that prepares him.

A dressage horse must always be ready to enter piaffe, even from the walk.

Don't start any exercise (in any gait) if the horse is not in good cadence and a good position. We must place the horse in the right conditions to execute the movements.

Basic rules: impulsion – correct position – fixity [*fixité,* stability of the poll and the base of the neck] – collection.

All lateral work begins with the hind-end.

It is through the variety of the exercises that the horse is suppled.

Be attentive to the cadence [of the horse] from the beginning [of dressage]. This will help you for the rest [of training].

Impulsion is a horse that stays "round as a ball," that remains in a given exercise with the same degree of energy without the continuous support of the aids.

We must not forget impulsion in the name of relaxation[75].

The hotter the horse, the more we must think about cadence, because he always wants to move too fast.

To increase impulsion through speed is an illusion. Speed cost us the loss of collection.[76]

We cannot say that a horse is trained until he is capable of starting into any gait (walk, trot, canter) from the halt, and halting from any exercise.

The standard of impulsion is not the speed, but the energy and vibration in which the horse works.

One of the secrets of collection is that the rein on the side of the bend must be a bit lighter than the other [outside] rein.

Try to get your horse to support himself in lightness in the trot with the minimum of aids.

In the short gaits, in order for the horse to engage [his hind legs], we need at least as much vibration as in the long gaits, maybe even more.

If the horse moves his poll, it is because the rider has lost control of something.

Before starting a movement, we must first establish the cadence and not start the movement however it may come. Therefore before starting a more advanced movement (at the trot for example), we must establish the cadence on a straight line. Then we can start the movement (a

75   *decontraction*

76   [This is true for trained horses, not so much for young horses learning to go forward, according to Nuno Oliveira own methodology for starting young horses]

69

shoulder-in for instance) with the same cadence [as we achieved on the straight line].

It is useful to close our eyes (particularly in the trot) for 2 or 3 strides, to really "become one" with the cadence.[77]

To achieve the head *placée* [placed: the correct *ramener* with the forehead on the vertical], the poll must be rounded.

We must always question [the quality] of the cadence and the lightness, and then take the opportunity to ask for an exercise, which means not to force it.

By developing the balance that we get the horse to go forward, not by making him trot or canter for hours on a loose rein.

Rule: to achieve [correct] transitions, we must do them when:

1. We have mastered the cadence,

2. We have the same level of energy [equal in all gaits]

3. We can be in *descente de main* [yielding of the hand] on the inside rein

We must obtain a horse that is round and light by the nuance and delicacy of our techniques, rather than by using "legs like a wrench" to obtain by force some flashy immediate effects.

Many riders, in the name of impulsion, put too much tension in their horses. Others in the name of lightness, have their horse "abandoned" [without a sufficient connection]. The truth [of equitation] is in between [those two extremes].

Look for the purity of the three gaits, the rest will come easily.

If you start a diagonal while letting the horse fall on the inside shoulder, you are losing impulsion.

There are two fundamental concepts:

1. We must not only activate the hind legs,

2. But also pay attention to the front end, to relax it and to have a pleasant and soft mouth.

To riders whose horse kicks or bucks in the trot:

A horse that bucks is obviously not trained. If he kicks, give him a series of *little* touches with the whip until he stops. Touch him on the thigh [above the stifle] and not on the belly. If needed, wiggle the reins and give him a little jerk. Even a little attack of the spur (a *"tic"*). Let me remind you that the leg must be relaxed before we use the spur.

Don't allow him to get into canter, or accelerate or run.

In the transitions walk – trot – walk - trot, the horse must keep his impulsion from trot to walk, so he doesn't lose his energy in the walk. He will need a walk with impulsion to go back to trot.

---

77   *se penetrer de la cadence*

If a horse resists, a good technique is to put him on a very small circle (of a diameter equal to the length of the horse's body) in a shoulder-in. Do a few circles by fixing the inside rein tightly, with a stronger contact on that rein. *However, here is a condition:* the exercise must not end up with the same contact that it started with. As it progresses, you must soften the fingers and reduce the contact.

It is not by trotting and cantering for miles that we will obtain a good trot and a good canter with a horse that doesn't lean on the hand. What is needed is to go back to the walk often and get the horse light in the walk, by varying the exercises and by "separating the force and the movement" [resolve the resistance of force in the walk or at the halt rather than during a stronger movement like the trot. This is a concept defined by Baucher]. This must be done while watching the regularity of the rhythm [tempo]. We lose the lightness if we don't pay attention to keeping the rhythm [tempo].

Collecting a horse consists of pushing, holding, releasing. When the horse is collected, we don't do anything anymore, we monitor it.

The quality of the gait we are going to ride depends on the quality of the gait we are in.

Impulsion is the maintenance of the energy in cadence. No impulsion without cadence and no cadence without impulsion.

If a horse doesn't put his nose on the ground when we ask, it means that he has not relaxed his back.

The difference between a collected horse and a compressed horse: the collected horse can put his nose on the ground while staying round.

If the poll is contracted, the medicine is the lateral flexion.

When a horse bends as easily to one side as the other at the request of either inside leg, then he is in balance.

Don't start an exercise if the position (of the head for example) is not correct.

A good way to control the tempo is to close our eyes and count (like a metronome). At the walk, count the four beats of the walk.

To a rider: don't think of lightness right now, think of impulsion and lightness will come. There are no horses that pull, only riders who allow pulling.

Lightness is when the horse doesn't lean on the hand, but stays round.

It is not by galloping a lot that we collect, it is by practicing many transitions walk – canter – walk.

Certainly, we must avoid the horse rushing, but also avoid the loss of energy, otherwise, the horse stops working.

Antoine rides Neptune at Xhoris, a four-year-old stallion and one of the first sons of Farsista (Alter Real).

Triggering the Passage.

One of the first things to do is the fixity of the front end. We can use the draw reins during a certain amount of time if necessary.

A horse must remain with his head "placed" [positioned on the vertical, the jaw relaxed, the neck round] otherwise he escapes [evades]. Lightness is only possible if the head is placed. Furthermore, we must be careful that the head doesn't move during the transitions.

The horse must remain consistent in the figures [of the manege].[78]

[Important] *note on the use for the draw reins:* the horse must not force against the draw reins, not lean on them. Their usefulness does not consist of placing the horse, it is rather to prevent the head from rising and moving around in the transitions. So we must adjust them, not to place the horse, but to start their action when the horse raises his head [keep the draw reins a few inches longer than the snaffle reins when the horse is in position]. Therefore we must hold the draw reins with the fingers, without grabbing it and without blocking the horse.

The other role of the draw reins is to give the horse the lesson "of the nose on the ground" to the young horses who tend to raise their neck too high and hollow their back. Therefore they are useful for not only [helping to secure] the *placer*, but also to lower the head.[79]

The three cornerstones of dressage are:
1) A constant position
2) A constant tempo [rhythm]
3) A constant vibration [degree of contained energy].

When [the horse] walks laterally, it must be in the same tempo than when he walks straight, therefore not any faster when he walks straight [the horse must not slow down when performing lateral work].

Remember: we must always start an exercise with good conditions to maintain an adequate degree of impulsion.

It is important to prevent the horse from leaning on the reins, otherwise he becomes rigid for the rest of the work.

Each horse has his own tempo and we need to work him in that particular tempo [to obtain the best results].

When the horse moves his head, loses fixity, he loses impulsion.

To practice exercises and movements with a horse that is not balanced, using force, is a catastrophe. What is needed is
1) the balance and

78   [A consistent position, a consistent rhythm/cadence, a consistent direction]
79   [WHILE LENGTHENING THE NECK. This action is achieved by an opening rein followed by a release of first, the outside rein, then the inside rein. It entices the horse to follow the sliding contact downward, seeking a connection]

2) the movements afterwards.

Impulsion can be defined as the ability by the horse to stay in the same cadence, the same position [*attitude*], with the same level of energy without the constant help of the rider.

To create a sequence of exercises, we must prepare each exercise and not surprise the horse.

The horse must learn to support himself [self carriage].

There are two designs of impulsion:

1) The one where the rider hits and prods the horse without end. This is the impulsion in which the rider carries the horse.

2) The true impulsion that results from the [intelligent sequences of] exercises that bring the horse to use himself.

The criteria of impulsion is not speed but the energy and vibration with which the horse performs.

In Latin equitation [dressage of French Tradition], [the use of] the legs precedes [the use of] the hand.

In Germanic equitation, [the use of] the hand precedes [the use of] the legs.

In Latin equitation, the hand must be a barrier that the horse must never overtake.[80]

In Germanic equitation, the hand acts first [by taking a contact] and the legs push against a hand that doesn't give [horse on the hand].

In the name of lightness, we shouldn't walk with abandoned reins [no contact] and a horse without impulsion. The great mistake about lightness is to have a horse ridden on floating reins neither round nor full of impulsion. This is not equitation, it is trail riding. We should only release [the contact] when the horse is round and in impulsion.

It is a mistake to say: "push the horse on the hand." I say: "balance your horse, so he can accept the hand, without leaning on it."

Sometimes riders confuse lightness with an abandoned horse.

Remember: before acting with the hand (for halting the horse for example), we always need to push [with the waist or the legs if needed].

To some students: "by resting the elbows on the rider's hips, the hands follow [the actions of] the waist and the torso. They play their role, but normally," [the actions of the hand is integrated with the actions of the body, rather than acting independently].

When a horse is going on the track of the arena [going large] *and becomes afraid of something that happens outside* or in the arena gallery, we must not use the outside rein to bring his nose forcefully back to the

80   [According to Baucher, the horse stays "a centimeter behind the hand - wherever the hand places him – and a mile in front of the legs," this is the concept of the "horse IN the hand"]

74

wall. We must bring his body back to the place where he has been frightened and only after that, his head. Therefore when riding on the left rein, the correction consists of doing a left shoulder-in to control [the position of] his body (and not his head). Use the left rein to put him in the left shoulder-in.

Another case that happened: [in a lesson of Nuno Oliveira], in which the shoulder-in was used, but with a different purpose than turning the horse's [head] away from what was scaring him. At [the riding school in] Xhoris, a horse shows a great fear of the gallery and absolutely refuses to go near it. It looks more like ill-will than [true] fear. Nuno Oliveira ask all the spectators to stand up and make as much noise as possible by stomping the floor, creating a major uproar and a strange spectacle (of humans standing and moving uncontrollably) for the horse. This may have been funny for the people, but certainly not for the horse. At every lap around the arena, the rider was asked to push the horse energetically in shoulder-in and try to get a few inches closer to the gallery (I cannot remember if it was in trot or canter, but certainly not in walk). After a few laps, the horse began accepting the situation and passed by the gallery. Back to walk, reward and patting.

The majority of horses have a concave side and a convex side. To perform an exercise like a shoulder-in for example, the language [of the aids] will be the same on both sides, but the dose of the aids will be different.

Remember: on the convex side, [for instance on the right side if the horse is naturally bent left] play with the rein [to lighten the contact], but don't pull, while trying to keep the contact on the other side [the left side]. The horse usually has a tendency to not take the contact on the concave side.

Note: a horse has less neck muscles on the concave side. If the rider pulls on the rein on the convex side, he will develop yet more muscles on that side by pulling and resisting. An endless fight will ensue.

Some comments on concavity and convexity: (let's consider a horse concave on the left side and convex on the right side). The concave side is apparently the easiest one because the horse naturally bends more easily on that side. In reality - for an educated, sensitive rider – it is the difficult side because, when the horse starts in trot on a left circle for example, the horse will have a tendency to load the outside shoulder (the right one) by placing his head to the left. There will be a tendency to throw the shoulders to the right against the wall. As a result, the rider will have to constantly replace the shoulders in front of the haunches [moving them to the left].

In the counter change of hand on two tracks, to change direction: [it is important to] put the inside leg in place [near the girth, close to the side], before bringing the outside leg back.

The less forceful aids are the most useful ones for [the development of] collection. The more a horse advances in his training and the more a rider advances in his or her knowledge, the more the legs replace the hands.

We place the horse in a diagonal position [encouraging the diagonal action of the horse's legs for the purpose of developing collection] by subtle lateral actions [rather than by direct, simultaneous diagonal actions of right hand and left leg for instance].

When we bring a horse back [downward transition within a gait] with semi-taught reins, we must be careful to do it without any jerkiness.

With a lazy horse, give a sharp and energetic attack of the spur, "an electric blow" and then keep the legs completely quiet, avoid continuously beating with the legs. If needed, repeat the exercise. After the blow, don't hold back with the reins, no contact; and let him run for a few steps, then slow him down smoothly. We must have aids (either legs or hands) ready to intervene at the precise moment, but not surprise the horse with a brusque movement.

To take a center line, we must always do it around the inside leg. To turn, we position the horse by the rein and then use the inside leg.

The legs must touch from back to front (not only for extensions). To push from back to front, we must push the buttocks forward, then the legs are in agreement with the torso.

Remember: we must resist when the horse resists and release when the horse releases. Do not release when the horse resists and do not release when he resists.

The leg starts from the hip and goes to the heel and the spur.

If the horse becomes crooked, we straighten him up by the outside rein, but we keep him straight with the legs.

Because all the exercises are for the purpose of suppling the horse, they must be obtained without force.

To turn, we don't pull on the inside rein, we keep both reins with equal tension. It is the outside shoulder that advances (compare this action with the bicycle handlebars).

Concerning lateral flexions.

First, do a square halt, ask for the direct flexion [mouth and poll] then ask for the lateral flexion. We need to practice the lateral flexions often with all horses. The horse must turn softly to the side, in lightness, with the mouth soft. If done otherwise, we bring his head to the side in resistance.

Sometimes it may be very important to ask for the complete lateral flexion, in order to obtain the complete submission of the horse.[81] But when we will use lateral flexion in further work (such as change of direction, two tracks, etc.), we should only ask for a very slight lateral flexion of the neck which will stay correctly positioned, along with the head. Understand that an exaggerated flexion would stop the impulsion by overloading the outside shoulder. As long as the jaw stays mobile, we achieve lightness and the lightest lateral indication will be sufficient for the changes of direction.

The suppling exercise that we call lateral flexion is nevertheless necessary because it consists of asking the most to secure the least [an extreme exercise used carefully]. We just need to know that in the following work, we will only ask for a slight bend of the neck with the condition that the head and neck is well-placed and importantly that the jaw remains relaxed.

---

81   [This is done at the halt generally, per Baucher]

Nuno Oliveira (left) teaching Antoine de Coux (right).

Chapter 4

EXERCISES, GAITS, TRANSITIONS,
CIRCLES, EXTENSIONS, SERPENTINES

In the circle, we must feel that we don't need to use the outside rein anymore than the inside rein. We need to feel the same intensity of contact in both.

Except when we do a circle [at one end of the school], we need to go into every corner. If we don't go into the corner, the horse might not be straight on the long side and float instead.

The more you enter into the corners, the more you dominate your horse.

The discipline of figures [geometry of the arena]. If the horse becomes crooked, it is because he is losing his impulsion and he is floating.

The horse uses himself more when he does accurate figures.

The circle is the major figure of the entire dressage. It is on the circle that we establish the tempo.

Serpentine in walk or trot: obtain the loops of the serpentine by the advancement of the outside shoulder, not because we mess with (pull on) the inside rein. It is the shoulders that give the direction. We turn [the horse] by the torso, not by the hand. And the horse turns around the inside leg. This leg must be close to the girth during the curve. We must prepare this curve and not surprise the horse. It is important that the horse not lose the cadence, that the trot changes and that the neck becomes too soft in every direction.

In short, we do the serpentine by advancement of the outside shoulder and support of the inside leg, and not by the movements of the hands.

In a serpentine, a very useful exercise, [we must keep the horse] in the same tempo and the same position [of the head and neck].

In a circle, the two reins must have an equal degree of tension and it is the outside shoulder that advances.

When we want to change rein through the diagonal, avoid the horse falling sideways. Therefore support the inside shoulder.

Don't always think about extending the gait, otherwise the horse may become hollow.

We must first relax [the horse] before doing an extension, so he can extend while in a state of relaxation.

The passing through the corner has many advantages
1) Impulsion on the straight line [that follows]
2) The beginning of a correct circle
3) The beginning of a shoulder-in or a half-pass
4) Also useful for [preparing] extensions, because the corner sits [the horse] more and engages the hind legs.

The serpentine is a precious exercise for the study of the feelings [that the horse gives to the rider]. We must feel that there is no more resistance on the left loop than on the right loop.

When working in the arena, we must often use the center line [to check that we have] a straight horse, because when we only follow the wall, we form illusions [on our straightness] and we do not learn to keep the horse straight.

On a circle, [we must achieve the] same tension on each side. Each time we do a circle, it is to improve something.

If, when doing a circle, you feel the same intensity of contact on the inside rein as on the outside rein, it is because the horse is busy doing a correct circle.

The serpentine of 3 or 4 loops is a useful exercise to verify if the horse is balanced equally on both sides.

On the center line, [when riding] a trained horse, we should have the feeling that the horse is ready to do a volte equally well to either side, at any moment.

In the transition from walk to trot, all the books say that the poll must stay at the same height. For me, I want more: I want *the horse to do the transition in the same state of mind.*

The transitions between gaits are good for every horse.
When you do a circle, it is not for the pleasure of walking around, it is to verify either the impulsion, or the cadence, or the fixity [of the head], or the position of the head.

On a circle, if you have too much inside rein, the horse puts the head to the inside and throws his haunches to the outside. He is not "on the circle" because his spine is not lined up with the arc of the circle.

Only perform transitions when the horse is not in resistance.
To have a light horse, we must help him want to detach his feet from the ground and not run forward.

When we start a trot extension on the diagonal, you must remember that at the end of the diagonal, you will need to go back to the slow trot with the same state of mind.

Trot extension: the rider must ask for it through a marked increase in impulsion established in the shorter gait that precedes. Again, it is all about preparing. Otherwise, if we prod[82] [with the spurs] during the extension: 1) the horse will become hollow and 2) the rider will not be able to sit as comfortably as if the horse had stayed round [in his top-line].

You cannot obtain good lateral movements if you are leaning forward, because [that position] puts too much weight on the forehand.

To a rider: during the loops [of a serpentine] your horse bends, that's good, but be careful that he doesn't bend too much. In other words: "think of the support of the outside rein" [to control the outside shoulder so it doesn't fall out].

Before starting lateral work (in walk or trot) such as shoulder-in, etc., first create the right cadence and the appropriate impulsion. So, before entering an exercise, verify the level of impulsion.

In lateral work, first think about the drive of the haunches, and then the bend comes progressively, not the other way round.

Lateral movements must be performed in a walk that is short and active.

It is useful to do tight movements [succession of lateral moves on circles in every direction] in order to make the horse more active in the larger movements.

When we do a lateral movement, we must get the feeling that it is initiated by the croup and not that the croup is lagging and the shoulders are starting [the lateral displacement].

We cannot say that a horse is trained if he is not capable of starting from the halt into any gait (walk, trot, canter) and into any exercise.

It is not by fighting a resistance in a straight line that we fix things. What is needed is to "bend"[83] the horse in every direction. It is the only way the rider has to be stronger than the horse. Go straight only after that is done.

Doing a very small circle is a good way to slow down the speed of the walk.

[Performing] an exercise is easy if it is the result of [the correct] preparation. It is the right preparation that really matters and is truly dif-

---

82   *pique*
83   *tordre*

ficult.

To a rider asking about the usefulness of the counter-shoulder-in: "It is a very effective way to work the difficult side of the horse. If it is the right side that is difficult (that offers less bend), we practice the counter-shoulder-in on that side."

In the lateral movements, give more importance to the haunches than to the bend. If the bend is excessive, it can put the horse in difficulty.

Even with a horse that knows complicated exercises, we must [often] come back to simple work [the basics].

In the travers to the right, the right leg 1) controls the bend and 2) helps maintain the impulsion.

Never let a horse that is resisting, walk on a straight line. Separate the force [resistance] from the movement[84] (Baucher).

In the saddle, we can canter more or less long, more or less short, even backwards. But on the lunge line, we always [ask the horse] to canter large, going forward [with ample strides].

To a rider: "If you don't insist that your horse does figures that are geometrically perfect, he will fall on one shoulder or the other and ends up [by being in charge and] doing what he wants.

No horse is trained if he cannot halt by the use of the spur, being from the walk, the trot or the canter and become immobile. No horse is trained if he is not obedient to the *effet d'ensemble. It is a basic lesson.*

For the halt on the spur (*effet d'ensemble*), the spur must be close to the girth and not further back.

Many riders are happy to get their horse tired by running around in the arena in trot and canter. This gets the horse tired. "Working a horse" is something else all together.

In lateral exercises, the more you get the haunches working, the more the weight is brought back. The more you let the horse go fast, the more the weight is on the shoulders. We must rule [the lateral exercises] by the use of the outside rein acting upwards and bringing the [rider's] outside shoulder back.

As I have said very often: to do a transition from one gait to another, we must prepare, which means

1) don't surprise [the horse] and

2) and first get the horse round and light.

We shouldn't rip the movements from the horse by force "to do things" in a bad position [and balance]. We must first work on the position and the relaxation of the horse's body. Performing movements in contrac-

---

84   [By halting the horse, resolving the resistance by a vibration or any other technique before resuming forward movement]

tion with a resistant horse is worthless.

Working a horse is not to perform the systematic repetition of the movements while fighting. [What is needed] is to first prepare the "attitude" [position and balance].

An extension is a displacement of the contact. We need to push [the horse] with the waist and the buttocks, not the legs.

L'effet d'ensemble [comprehensive effect] is a way to round the horse's [top-line], to dominate him, but also to get him more forward.[85]

Comment: *L'effet d'ensemble* is not indicated when the horse is not truly forward.

A horse becomes more supple by the repetition of appropriate exercises [practiced in relaxation].

I have often said that an exercise must be prepared. It is fundamental that the horse be relaxed. But this is particularly important when we begin to study a new exercise. It cannot be forced.

In an exercise, the passage for instance, we must not go beyond what the horse can give. But within the limits of what he can give, we must demand regularity [in the cadence and the level of performance].

If at the end of an exercise, we are still using the same intensity of aids, it is because the horse has not released, or simply, that he has not understood [the demand].

It is by [working the horse] through different exercises in the same bend that we can often supple up the horse on the difficult side.

For example (in walk or trot) go several times from the shoulder-in [right] on a circle, to another circle with haunches-in (same bend), until there is no longer any resistance on the inside rein.

After a defense [spook, etc.], put the horse back immediately where the defense occurred.

Conditions of a good lateral flexion [in place]:

1) First [insist] on a square halt

2) Then place the horse in a good position of *ramener* [forehead on the vertical]. First obtain a direct flexion [release of jaw and poll] before asking for a lateral flexion.

3) [Make sure] that the horse does not overload one lateral pair (left lateral pair [of legs] if asking for left flexion).

4) Insist on a relaxed mouth. Without first obtaining the relaxation of the jaw, the flexion is worthless. The horse must release the jaw, the poll and the neck.

The horse must move [his head and neck] softly to the side in com-

---

85   [Because this roundness facilitate the forward movement after the *effet d'ensemble*]

plete lightness, with the mouth soft. Otherwise we are bringing the head to the side in resistance.

On the lunge: The horse cannot make the circle on his own. The [hand which holds the] lunge must not pull and [the lunge] must be slightly tight without undue force - an elastic tension. The lunge is your hand and the whip is your leg. [They should be used in] the "accord of the aids" [coordination of the aids]. If the horse comes inside the circle by himself, it usually means that he is lacking impulsion.[86] Additionally, the horse shouldn't halt by himself. It is the handler who must halt him. Also, the gaits must be regular. If the horse moves his head or doesn't yield [to the side reins], use a vibration of the wrist [shiver]. Watch the horse's feet and see if they have energy and good cadence. Just as much as he shouldn't come to the inside of the circle on his own, he shouldn't break the canter and fall back into trot either. Push him back into canter immediately.

When we go through a corner at the walk in shoulder-in, we need to support the shoulders a little and make the haunches walk a little more. In effect, the [haunches] have to cover more ground.

If we let the horse run, he rushes and covers less ground [with each stride]. He [ends up] doing more strides (in all three gaits).

One of the great utilities of the work-in-hand, is that we can get the horse to take some [working] positions without the weight of the rider [impeding him].

When we lunge with a *Chambon*, we must stay in walk and trot and lunge in a quiet manner, not in a quick pace, use a slow rhythm so the horse can relax his back. Do many transitions trot – walk – trot, all with a slow trot.

When the horse walks straight, it must be without resistance. He must therefore walk in balance, with an ample gesture [of the horse's legs], and "giving his back" [relaxing it].

Practice shows us that it is always useful to work beforehand with relaxed lateral work. For instance, working the horse in the same bend in three different exercises: circle in shoulder-in, volte with haunches-in [in half-pass position] and counter-shoulder-in.

---

86   [The horse usually falls out of the circle on one side – most often the left – and falls in the circle – most often the right. It is due to the innate asymmetry of his balance. The falling on one shoulder must be corrected by the action of the lunge hand (bringing the horse in on one side and sending him away by making little waves with the lunge toward him the other direction). The straight position is then confirmed by the effect of impulsion. This is what was observed in Nuno Oliveira lunging practice]

84

Enlarging and making the circle smaller in shoulder-in (on a spiral) is a useful exercise.

Ride all the different exercises in a sequence.

For the exercise: "trot – halt – reinback – trot," only do short reinbacks and start forward as soon as the weight is noticeably back on the hind legs.

For the transitions trot – canter – trot (in particular when dealing with a lazy horse), create first the necessary vibration [energy] in the trot.

It is a good technique to return to shoulder-in, when faced with tension.

We must start the exercises by the haunches.

If a horse puts his head too far inside [of the circle or shoulder-in], he throws his weight on the outside shoulder.

The bend, the stiff, concave and convex sides.

Example of a horse that is convex on the left side; he [naturally] bends right. [When going on] the left rein, his tendency will be to have too much weight on the left side and to resist on that side.

Remedy: left rein lighter than the right (the left side will [always] be the difficult side), but without forgetting to keep the contact with the right rein. Use continuous vibration upwards on the left rein the entire life of the horse. To bend him left, replace the [action of the] left rein by the [action of the] left leg near the girth. [Use the calf, not the spur. This will correct the problem at its source which is the deviation of the rib cage to the left].

When the horse misses an exercise – a flying change for instance – [the spirit of] discipline demands that we ask again in exactly the same place.

Entering correctly in the corners helps the horse to become consistent in his gait.

The *effet d'ensemble* [comprehensive effect] must be started early with horses who are truly forward. It must be started not so soon with horses who lack sufficient nervous influx.

All the exercises (halt, reinback, circle, shoulder-in, half-pass, etc.) are designed to render the horses more flexible. Afterwards, they can travel straight in flexibility and not in rigidity.

With a horse who doesn't have a natural extension, we must not force him to extend before he has become sufficiently seated [on his haunches], because the risk is to hollow his back.

What is a good circle? One in which the horse correctly bends on the arc of the circle, keeping his cadence without dropping a shoulder or a haunch outside [the line of the circle].

Chapter 5

THE WORK IN WALK AND TROT

If the walk is "sleepy," the horse will start a sleepy trot that is open [the opposite of collected]. Prepare the walk so the horse departs in the trot with the minimum of aids.

The collected walk is short, slow and with a clear cadence [in which you can hear the steps distinctly from each other]. Listen to the cadence of your walk: 1—2 —3—4—

If the horse doesn't sit in the walk, he will not depart seated in the canter, instead he will rush forward [into the canter].

A collected walk must have distinct steps, be majestic like a "church walk," and nothing is majestic that is rushed.

The walk requires less effort from the horse [than the trot or canter] and it allows him to think.

In walk, it is useful to close your eyes for three or four strides and count [the footfalls]. It helps us feel if the strides are equal.

If we use the spur during the walk, the horse will rush his walk.

The entire lateral work, particularly in the walk, must be done in a very distinct cadence [a slow tempo].

A collected walk cannot be quick. It must be slow and mark the four distinct beats of the walk.

If the horse rushes his walk in the lateral work, we need give him more support [from the hand].

We must pay attention to the purity of the mechanics of the walk. A good walk is a round walk in which the limbs land one after the other in a relaxed manner.

In the walk, try to achieve the maximum of energy within the slowness of the gesture.

The collected walk is the slowest walk possible with the most energy.

The mechanics of the walk is the closest to the mechanics of the canter. Therefore, do not always practice the transitions: "walk – trot – canter," but the reverse: "walk – canter – trot." We do not maintain the extension of the walk by the spurs or the legs, but by the [action of the] waist.

To a student: if your horse "holds back" in the walk, do a few trot strides to get the horse thinking forward again and return to the walk afterwards.

It is when we walk on a loose rein that we let the horse extend the walk.

In the walk, it is useful to link three exercises: the circle, the corner and the shoulder-in.

The reason why we need *a short* [and slow] *walk* to work the horse. Mechanics of the walk: right front, left hind, left front, right hind (four beat gait).

In the walk, the front legs start before the hind legs. It is the only gait in which the front legs start first. In trot, the [front and hind legs of a diagonal pair] start together and in the canter, the hind legs start first.

If we work in a large walk, there is more time between the landing of the front legs and the hind legs and the horse is not "on the ball."[87]

Medium trot does not consist of going faster [in a quicker tempo], but rather staying in the same rhythm while doing larger strides, without running, in more or less the same cadence.

The usefulness of all the trot exercises (circles, shoulder-in, etc.) is revealed when it all happens in the same trot.

To perform a series of exercises at the trot [lateral exercises on short turns], we need to be in a short trot that is very active.

The extension of trot on the diagonal must begin in balance and not on the forehand, so don't lean forward, even in posting trot, and control [the equilibrium of the horse].

The extended trot is also a collected trot. But instead of just going upward, it also goes forward.

The aids for the walk pirouette:

When the horse knows the half-pass, the half-pirouette is simple to achieve.

Put the horse in collected walk on the long side. Turn across the arena. Hold the horse back [by an upward support of the hand] and push [by advancing the waist] to put the horse "on the ball" in the walk.

At the moment of starting the pirouette, relax arms and legs without losing the contact. Therefore "give" at that moment.

If in a left pirouette, put a little weight on the left buttock, support the horse with the left leg and bring the right leg slightly back.

Subsequent explanation of Nuno Oliveira: alternate left leg and right leg.

87   [Rounded in his top line]. [Long walk with a lot of over-stride have a tendency to lateral timing of the footfalls. Nuno Oliveira is referring to the fact that the collected walk has a very slight diagonal tendency (landing of diagonal pairs slightly closer than in the free walk)]

One of the secrets of the walk half-pirouette, is the activity of the walk before you start. You need more legs than hand to create the pivot. Don't stay attached to the mouth, light hands.

Do not stop [the forward motion] between the straight line and the beginning of the pirouette. If the horse knows the half-pass, the pirouette is a simple thing. Establish a collected walk on the long wall. Hold and push to put the horse "on the ball" at the walk. For the left half - pirouette. Relax the arms and legs. Start the half-pirouette with the inside seat and the inside (left) leg. Put the weight on the left buttock. Then without losing the contact, use the right leg and right rein and alternate the effects of the legs: left leg – right leg – left leg – right leg. Go from one leg to the other as quickly as possible, without blocking with the hands, so the horse doesn't ground the inside hind foot when it is pivoting. For a horse that finds the walk half-pirouettes difficult, prepare him by doing some short reinbacks, and when you feel him round, advance a couple of steps and do the half-pirouette without a bend and more by using the legs than the hands.

Voltes around the haunches [small circles quarters-in/haunches-in].

It is necessary for the [movement of the] outside shoulder to "wrap" itself around the entire body of the horse, so the weight doesn't remain on this outside shoulder. When we perform a circle around the haunches, if the shoulders don't stay in front of the haunches, the inside hind leg goes wide toward the inside of the circle instead of engaging itself. The outside shoulder must "cover," "wrap" itself around the inside of the horse. So in a circle around the haunches to the right, if the left shoulder stays too much to the left, the weight remains on that left shoulder and the right hind leg will have some difficulty in engaging under the body. The rider must feel that the horse keeps his weight on the inside hind leg (right hind). If you don't send the left shoulder to the right, the inside hind leg (right), instead of coming under, runs the risk to open to the right side.

Because of the [different] mechanics of the walk and trot:

In walk: the lateral work must be done in a tempo that is slow [and in which you can hear each footfall distinctly], otherwise the horse will overload the outside [of the bend].

In trot: [the lateral work] can be done in any tempo [that suits the horse's natural gaits], but [the lateral exercises] must not reduce [the amplitude of] the trot by the fact that the horse is displacing himself sideways.

For going from collected to medium trot, the horse should open the stride without running.

In the lateral movements in the trot, do not let the horse reduce his trot [stride], because then, he would lose the engagement [of his hind legs].

One of the secrets of trot extensions (on the diagonal for example) resides in the manner in which we perform the corner (the second corner of the short side). [Nuno Oliveira advises to take corners quite deep and with a fraction of a shoulder-in to balance the horse and engage him].

Cadence of the trot: it must not be rushed, but rather slow and active, which doesn't necessarily mean short [strided].

If you let the horse run at the trot, he will lose all his collection.

Study of the transition from halt to trot.

1) In preparation, the halt must be square and sharp, with the weight on the hocks.

2) That the horse doesn't lean on the hand, maintain a soft, elastic contact. The reins cannot be too taught.

3) That the movement [into trot] starts from the hind legs.

4) No [involuntary] raising of the poll, however small it might be.

When travelling on a straight line, if we feel that the horse is not completely straight, swing the hands very lightly from left to right and right to left, in order to oppose the shoulders to the haunches [by bringing the shoulders in front of the haunches], and cease [this motion] when you feel him [becoming] straighter.

For the transition from walk to trot, pay attention to straightness, to cadence, to the fixity [of the neck, base and poll] and also to impulsion, so the horse departs from the hind-end and not the front-end.

To return to collected trot after the medium trot, use the waist without pulling on the reins.[88]

Return to the medium trot from the collected trot while maintaining the same tempo.[89]

In a circle, [make sure that] the horse doesn't press on the inside shoulder.

And foremost, feel both buttocks move forward in equal fashion left and right, and not on one side only.

---

88   [Using the torso to "take" on the movement by tightening the waist very briefly]

89   [Some horses will resist the maintenance of the cadence by using a faster tempo (many Iberians with bullfighting breeding), others will resist by slowing down to passage tempo (many warm bloods with a lot of suspension). Both tendencies must be corrected].

90

Walk serpentine: is useful for developing the regularity of the walk[90]. In the walk, you must hear four beats.

The quality of the walk determines the quality of the gait that follows (trot or canter).

The walk is a gait that helps us make the horse accept many things [Baucher]. Afterward, we must start the trot, which is more effective [to develop the dynamic athleticism of the horse – La Guérinière].

For a good walk:
1) Count four equal beats: 1-2-3-4
2) and feel the back walk [swing] with [the movement of] the legs.

When we are in the circle at the walk, we must not have the feeling that there is one shoulder and one haunch on the outside and one shoulder and one haunch on the inside, but that the entire horse is in the circle.

The preliminary condition for a good halt depends on whether the horse is well-collected.

The quality of the walk: constant tempo – constant position (of the head and poll) and constant energy. In other words: "collection." [Insist on] the purity of the mechanics of the walk.

Feeling that the horse is straight is feeling that he is not falling on the right shoulder nor the left shoulder nor on the right haunch nor the left haunch.

Straight horse:
1) Straight [symmetrical] in his ears, shoulders and croup;
2) Straight not only visually, but also in the sensation [he gives to the rider]. For that to happen, the horse cannot be rigid.

Before passing from walk to trot, create already in the walk the vibration of the trot. Therefore, to go from walk to trot:
1) Develop an adequate walk.
2) Then, ask for trot with the softest aids possible, in order not to surprise the horse.

This is the best way to obtain a horse that is balanced at the trot.

Usefulness of the corner (if it is well done) [deep with a good bend and a slight shoulder-in]:
1) In walk, each time, the horse will sit slightly.
2) In canter, the corner is an opportunity to improve the balance.

If we depart into trot from a reinback, the weight must remain on the haunches [during the depart], and the horse must depart directly into trot without an intermediate stride of walk. There must not be any inter-

---

90   [and its symmetry by extending alternately the gesture of each lateral pair when they are placed on the outside of each of the turns]

Antoine riding Fauno in Uccle in 1975, at the Musette Riding School.

ruption between the reinback and the depart to trot.

In the trot variations, we must teach the horse to obey [the effects of] the rider's weight. For example, go from posting trot to sitting trot on the short side of the arena to shorten the trot, not by using the reins, but by [slowing] the torso.

For the collected trot and the medium trot: same height of the poll/head, but forehead slightly less vertical in the medium.

In extended trot, give [the reins] a little, but not too much, otherwise the horse becomes unbalanced and falls on the forehand.

In a circle, the rider must not be moved to the left or the right. One must stay within the axis of the horse. So, bring the outside shoulder forward a little (idea of the bicycle handlebar).

In trot, pay attention that the poll always stays at the same height. The [correct] passing through the corner is important to start the long side with a collected horse.

In trot, keep the waist supple, otherwise the body will be roughed up [by the movement of the horse's back] and the hand will also be shaken, preventing it from being fixed. [The fixed position of the hand is in relation to the horse's back].

In the serpentine, in each loop, touch [the horse] delicately near the girth with the inside leg when you are turning.

In the trot serpentines, pay attention to the fact that the horse must bend as much to one side as the other with each of the turns and that the trot remains unchanged.

When the horse has a trot that lacks impulsion, [his back] will become hollow.

The success of the work on the serpentine (like flying changes or passage) is based on the [performance of perfect] geometry.

In a serpentine, the horse must turn by the play of the rider's shoulders and not by a traction on the reins.

In a good trot, [the feet of the horse] *must detach from the ground* [with energy] *and not only push forward horizontally in a "shaving"*[91] [daisy cutting] *trot.* Therefore, only depart into trot when the weight [of the horse is slightly] on the haunches.

In walk or in trot, what is needed is to feel energy in the slowness [of the gait].

To a rider: when your horse starts the passage-like, hovering trot, that hollows the back, chase the haunches to the outside [into lateral work].

The true extended trot is done from the moment when the horse

---

91   *rasant*

has put his weight well on the haunches. Then the hind legs will push during the extension.

When we take the diagonal in medium trot, we must avoid that the horse runs or rushes, so we can return to the collected trot easily, without effort.

In the "little"[92] collected trot, the horse must maintain his vibration and not fall asleep.

The good extension is one in which the horse starts energetically from the beginning. [It is successful] because he has been properly prepared. Instead, if the horse falls on the forehand after a few strides, he has not been prepared and the rider is pushing during the extension.

The half-pirouette in trot is not an easy exercise. We must start the trot as if the horse were going to piaffe. It must be done nearly in piaffe (it is one of the exercises of the "Square of La Guérinière").

In the little counter-changes of hand at the trot [half-pass left to half-pass right to half-pass left] we must pay attention to the symmetry [of the exercise] and to keep the same tempo. They are a good preparation for the trot extensions.

We must never start into trot by increasing the speed of the walk. Therefore it is the vibration that must increase, without altering the position, the speed nor the tempo.

In the trot extension, the horse must have suspension, but must not run.

Don't start into trot before the horse is correctly positioned [head and neck] in the walk.

With a hot horse full of impulsion, the problem of the trot extension on the diagonal is to know how to slow him down at the end of the diagonal. If he rushes, it's not going to work.

Only start the trot or the canter when the horse has relaxed his body at the walk. And if there is a resistance, return to walk.

With a horse in resistance, use the posting trot. If the horse releases, sitting trot. If needed (in case of a new resistance), return to posting trot. And if needed, return to walk to compose things.

In trot, we must feel that the horse "springs off the ground" by his energy. Feel that he jumps upward and not forward.

Preparation of the extended trot:

1) Increase the impulsion, the energy of the trot, make it "bubbly." [thus - full of energy and life, like Champagne].

2) Prevent the horse from running, even diminish his speed.

---

92   [In French "petit trot" is a very short trot used in the French dressage tradition to develop obedience and maneuverability with a light contact]

3) Prevent him from falling on the inside shoulder [in the second corner of the short side] when he starts the extension on the diagonal.

If a horse doesn't have a natural trot extension, if he doesn't have movement, he must at least have some suspension in his extension.

Actual case: after several attempts, a young lady rider says that she cannot create sufficient energy to obtain an extension and declares that she is tired. Nuno Oliveira: "I am going to make you do an extension without getting tired. Get into a halt. Give the horse a series of little taps with the whip without letting him move off. Wait until he gets his head in place [*ramené* position] and that he has become "bubbly." [Now], get into trot, extend." [De Coux doesn't mention if it was successful, but we can guess quite surely that Nuno Oliveira's technique worked].

A "unified" trot, as the classic authors used to say, is the trot in which the horse maintains, on his own:

1) The same position
2) The same speed
3) The same dose of energy.

To teach the reinback, at the beginning help the horse understand the movement by simple means, such as ground work for example.[93]

Preliminary condition for a good reinback: a straight horse.

[In the reinback, once the horse is trained], the horse must not pass through the halt or immobility [between forward and backward movement]. He must stay in movement. It is a swing from forward to backward. First increase the impulsion (like for the halt). Then stop the forward march. Then by the use of the weight[94] and the legs, give a backwards direction.

The true trot is the one in which the horse keeps his cadence without the use of hand or legs aids, the only [active] aid being the waist.

In the serpentine, pay attention to the fact that the neck bends equally in both directions.

Each time you pass the corner correctly, you improve the balance of the horse.

---

93   [The handler stands in front of the horse and taps on his ankles or his knees in time with the lift of each foot while acting on the reins in the direction of the reinback. Reward every step with the voice and a caress at every stage of the training. Later on, the handler stands behind the shoulders while holding the reins over the withers and repeats the reinback until the reinforcement of the whip action is no longer necessary. In the next stage, the handler from the ground helps the rider to obtain the reinback from the saddle by first standing close to the horse and progressively further and further until the help is no longer needed. -J.P.G.]
94   [torso coming back]

At the moment of the depart into trot, you need to have the feeling that the hind legs are pushing the horse forward. There should be no movements of the poll.

In the trot circle, don't allow the horse to throw his weight on the outside shoulder.

Transition walk – trot: we must get a sensation [that goes] from back to front as well as upwards, and not have poll movements that hollow the back. The horse must start the trot from the hind-end and not throw his head up.

Respect the geometry of the figures: a circle is a curved line with a constant bend throughout.

In the serpentine, prepare the turns with the torso and not by the reins, especially not the inside rein. In the serpentine, it is not the inside rein that pulls, it is the outside shoulder that advances. In this way of proceeding, there is also a [small] action of the inside rein, but it is much softer and more nuanced. At the same time that the [rider's] outside shoulder advances, slightly load the tread of the inside stirrup.

In a circle at the walk, don't let the horse throw his forces [weight] neither to the inside nor the outside; have the sensation that you are sitting in the axis of the horse.

When a horse cuts the arena[95], for instance on the center line A to C, he must remain at the same speed.

We cannot collect a horse that walks rapidly. We need to be in the appropriate walk.

It is not possible to do a good transition from walk to trot if the walk is hollow and not collected. We need a slow walk, with a poll that flexes and a lifted back, the head staying in the same position; in short, a horse that stays "round in his walk."

In a circle (at the walk for example), if you have too much inside rein, the head will be too much to the inside and the horse will put the weight of his shoulders to the outside.

In a volte [small circle] on two tracks with quarters-in at the walk, to the right, we must feel that the right hind leg progresses [engages forward].

In collected trot, we need:
1) The head and the poll to be the highest point.
2) The hind legs truly engaged
3) A moment of suspension.
Try to have a trot that is "detached from the ground" and not daisy

---

95   *fait un doubler*

cutting.[96]

"Horse in hand": Academic Equitation starts by the horse coming in the hand[97]. It is not the rider that creates that connection by pulling [on the reins], it is the horse that must seek the contact with the hand.

The forehead must be vertical and the horse remains light. The "horse in hand," is the horse well-placed [positioned], rounded [flexion of the poll], in impulsion and in self-carriage. Then, just add the aids, the mouth being relaxed [release of the jaw].

The horse takes the contact himself. The horse "grows" in front, elevates and takes the position. Then he becomes light.

He has engaged his hind legs, rounded his back and established the contact with the hand, becoming as light as his sensitivity allows [the word "finesse" used by Nuno Oliveira defines the degree of innate responsiveness proper to each horse].

In canter, the horse in hand (*mise en main*) means that he keeps the same head position, the same cadence, the same speed, the same dosage of energy, the same degree of contact.

The horse on the hand [*Cheval sur la main*]:

1) The hand must always be in communication with the mouth of the horse;

2) But it is necessary that the horse, solicited by the legs, takes the contact himself.

The hand must not come backward to seek the mouth. From there comes the necessity of light contact.

If the horse keeps the same height of the poll and the same degree of flexion of the poll, it is one proof of collection [necessary but not sufficient, he must also engage his hind legs]. If the horse, during any transition between exercises or between gaits, changes the height of his poll or gives little movements of the poll, it means that he is neither forward nor collected.

If the circle is not regular, it is because the horse is floating. A circle is a curve with a constant bend, not an hexagon.

The technique for riding a circle is to advance the outside shoulder without losing the contact of the outside rein or pulling on the inside rein. It is the principle of the "bicycle handlebar." Same principle applies for the serpentine.

We can consider the walk to be collected when it gains in height and loses in length.

96   *rasant*
97   *mise en main* [soft connection with the reins, with the forehead on the vertical]

The torso must accompany [the balance and movement of the horse] or oppose it [according to the needs of the moment].

In principle the rider's shoulders must remain parallel to the horse's shoulders. Except in the case [when the horse creates a] resistance, in which case, we must quickly invert [the position of the rider's shoulders].

Be as quick to caress [pat and reward] as to correct.

To see if the horse is walking straight, fix your eyes on a faraway point. If the ears are not at the same level, it means that the head is not straight.[98]

Halt: if the horse becomes crooked, if you prod him with the spurs, he will halt in rigidity. We must try to halt [through the action of] the torso. He must halt straight, in peace, without resistance, from back to front, with the horse in the hand and not "open."[99] In the halt, we must not let the head get high [above the bit]. [After the halt, the horse] must start again without becoming crooked and without lifting the head, with walk steps in a regular rhythm 1—2—3—4 .

If we use too much inside rein, we will never have a straight horse.

The legs [of the rider] must be independent one from the other. When we use one leg, the other one must stay quiet.

The leg must not be too far forward nor too far back, (baring exceptional cases). It must simply be "descended" [made longer without forcing and without gripping].

On a circle, if we do too many things with the inside rein, the horse throws his weight to the outside, and the horse will not be "in the circle."

The abuse of the spur can have a double effect, according to the temperament of the horse:

1) It might get the horse dull if he is the lazy type;

2) It might get him excited and make him rush if he is sensitive [*fine*] and nervous.

What is the "adjustment of the reins?" It is establishing a soft contact.

At the beginning of your lesson, adapt the intensity of your aids to the mood of your horse.

We don't do a circle just for going around, but to increase the horse's balance, impulsion, position and cadence.

When you are doing an exercise like a circle or a half-pass, etc., it is not the horse you must look at, it is the trajectory you are planning to follow and the point where the horse should arrive.

98   [This usually reflects other unevenness in the body, such as the loading of the shoulders. This is why it is important to correct it]

99   [without *ramener*/forehead on the vertical; the opposite of collected]

98

If the contact is excessive, the horse will pull, if the contact is too weak, the horse will float.

We must hold the whip resting on the thigh pointing toward the horse's hind-end and not toward the horse's shoulder.

Try to intrigue with the discretion of your aids. That the spectator asks himself or herself: "how can this rider obtain such a result without [apparently] doing anything?." To achieve that, we must prepare the exercises, for example, by sitting the horse before the flying change.

The torso of the rider works like the fulcrum of a old fashion scale and it can used, at will, to place weight on one tray (the forehand) or the other (the hind-end).

A circle is a line of constant curvature, and it is necessary that the horse's spine be adapted to the curve of that [particular] circle.

Don't forget that in the transitions, we must keep the horse round.

Importantly, when doing a downward transition, you must not abandon [the contact] but push [with the waist]. For example, to go from canter to trot, the horse must grow in front when he begins the trot.

Often, riders want to obtain "things" [advanced movements] too soon, and even if the horse can do "these things," you need to go back to walk – trot – canter and not lose sight of the purity of the three gaits.

When starting from the halt, don't let the horse go with the head down [or out, "open"].

When taking the center line, do not alter the speed.

For the transitions collected trot – medium trot – collected trot, pay attention to three things:

1) Stable position of the poll,

2) Keep the cadence of each trot identical,

3) Return to the collected trot by the torso and not by the hands.

Principle: Pay attention to the fixity of the front end in the transitions, otherwise it is proof of a lack of impulsion.

Insistence on the necessity of paying close attention to the quality of transitions.

The rider's legs should travel neither forward nor back (except for particular cases), rather they should be simply descended [down].

In a good trot, the horse must be relaxed and each step must be equal to the next.

If you bother the horse [incessant actions of the aids], the trot will be spoiled. It is when the tempo is the slowest, without the horse reducing his speed, that the trot is the best. Then the horse detaches himself from the ground.

Chapter 6

CANTER WORK

The quality of the canter depends on the quality of the walk [or trot] that precedes it.

Canter with a young horse: first ride with long reins without planning to collect him (see the chapter on "young horse").

In a cadenced canter, we must feel that the horse engages his hind legs, that it is a canter from back to front.

If the horse starts a circle in canter without impulsion, he will have a tendency to lean in the circle.

In the circles in canter, don't sit on the outside.

In the circles in canter, feel the same intensity of contact left and right and don't have the inside rein without contact.

In canter, we must not be rigid, not necessarily too elegant. What is needed is to "go with the horse." It is the waist that must become soft and the torso should not do too much [not pumping back and forth with the shoulders].

When performing changes of direction, if the horse puts too much weight on the inside shoulder, give him more support on that side.

It is necessary that the horse starts his canter mentally calm, and not in panic.

With a horse that panics in the canter, ask for many transitions trot – canter – trot – canter, without departing into the canter from the walk. And get into canter when you feel that the trot is relaxed enough.

In the canter, you must feel that the horse *bascules* [rocking motion around an axis placed under the rider].

After an extended canter, return to the collected canter through the action of your torso, not by the hands.

We must slow the canter by the waist, not by the hands.

Don't try to shorten the canter [collected canter] before obtaining an active medium canter.

In the canter, we don't need a static position [rigid body]. But we shouldn't move any more than the horse moves either. We need to move as much as the horse does, accompany him, not more.

In the transition from canter to walk, perform it so that the horse does not take intermediate trot strides, because that puts him on the forehand. But this is only possible if the horse is collected.

We must not depart into canter from a walk that is too open [not collected enough].

When doing counter-canter, be careful that the horse does not increase his speed and change his cadence when he is on the short side [of the arena].

The canter is a succession of three jumps and each jump contains the following one.

The qualities of a good canter: round, with impulsion, straight, cadenced, light.

Don't try to cadence the canter of a horse that is not collected, because you risk diminishing the impulsion. Don't try to place a horse at the canter [position his head] before he has achieved a good position and self-carriage in the trot.

For a horse to have good bascule in the canter [uphill rocking motion], the horse needs to be straight. Therefore avoid bending him [too much]. It is the outside rein that keeps the horse straight by placing the shoulders in front of the haunches.

At the canter, we must not perform exceptional rein actions: the outside rein acts parallel to the body of the horse. To conserve the cadence of the canter, it is important that the horse's shoulders be well-placed [straight in front of the haunches].

In the canter, if the rider moves minimally, the horse can cadence himself better.

Canter so that, if you release the reins, the horse doesn't increase his speed. This requires a relaxed canter with a good bascule.

If your horse has a tendency to rush his canter, play with the reins, don't block a single rein: take the left rein, release the right rein, take the right rein, release the left, take both reins, release them both. Vary the contact.

In the canter circle, keep your shoulders parallel to the horse's shoulders. Therefore, advance the outside shoulder. And load the inside stirrup, particularly in the corners to help the horse.

Remember the importance of the outside rein in the canter. It is the one that straightens the horse and helps him sit.

Counter-canter on the short side:

With a young horse, bend him toward the center of the arena [bend with the turn]. As his collection increases, progressively bend him the other way.[100]

100   [This is a fundamental teaching of Nuno Oliveira that differentiates him, quite rightly, from other authors. This method of teaching counter-canter is applicable to horses just starting dressage and gives them huge benefits in the

102

In a canter circle, reduce the size of the circle mostly by the outside rein and enlarge the circle by the use of the inside rein.

Too much inside rein in the canter makes the horse brace to the inside. If in the canter to the right the horse is not straight and keeps his haunches to the right, the more you use the right rein and place the head to the right, the more he will place his haunches to the right. It is the left rein you need to use to place the shoulders in front of the haunches and then go back to the track.[101]

In the canter, if the rider bounces in the saddle, he cannot collect the horse. The more we bounce in the saddle, the more the horse gets nervous.

In the *canter half-pass*, the horse must not modify his canter and increase his speed.

In the canter, if your legs are too far forward and your waist is not relaxed enough, you will end up bouncing in the saddle. Sliding the buttocks toward the front of the saddle is only possible if your waist is relaxed and your legs [hang] without contraction.

In the counter-canter on the long side, the horse must remain parallel to the wall and not push the haunches to the outside.

In the *canter depart*, the torso of the rider must not lean forward: that would be a mistake because a depart involves raising of the forehand.

To turn on the center line in canter, the gaze of the rider must be fixed on the line the horse is going to trace. On the center line, fix a distant point forward. As the turn comes, again trace it by looking at it a little ahead of time. It is a way to say that the weight [of the rider] must be in agreement with the movement.

Obviously, the canter depart must occur without the horse lifting his poll at the moment of the depart.

In the canter, make sure that the horse keeps the same speed, the same position and develops the same dose of energy. That is impulsion.

To pass from canter to walk, lift the torso and release the contact immediately without pulling continuously on the reins.

If you feel some "resistance of weight" when in the canter, bring your shoulders back (moving the "fulcrum of the scale") and make sure that your hands follow your torso.[102]

If your horse rushes:

_____

early development of the balance in canter, as well as creates a lot of reach on the side of the lead (outside of the turn). This increased reach can then be used to prepare the medium trot by doing transitions from counter-canter to trot at the beginning of the long side]

101   [by pushing the horse forward with the inside leg]

102   [in effect doing a half-halt]

Advance the waist and grow the torso while tightening the fingers for an instant, but without the hands pulling or moving back.

Few horses can resist this braking effect of the torso.

With a horse that has a tendency to open in the canter [lose collection], we must first practice some exercises to get him rounder (shoulder-in) and increase his balance to make him more lofty (piaffe sessions).

With a horse who has a tendency to "ball up" too much [stays too round and refuses to gain a bigger stride], we must stretch him by doing some extended canter in a more open frame.

Absolute principle:

Each time in the canter that the horse *wants to change his speed or rush* the tempo, we must give support to the canter and the cadence:

1) By bringing the outside shoulder back and by using an upward movement of the waist. (To act upwards, the hand doesn't necessarily need to be moving, it is a question of placing the wrist).

2) And by playing with the inside rein, just as if you held a flower in your hand. It is necessary for the inside rein to be in a loop for short moments.

By slightly lifting the outside rein while bringing the outside shoulder back and by using a movement of the waist [waist forward and torso erect], we can send the weight back [on the haunches]. However, the head of the horse must remain straight, so in the left canter the head must not turn to the right.[103]

When we release the left rein (in the left canter), we must support the horse on the right side[104] until the horse is corrected, then we can release both reins.

On the resisting side: when the horse pulls on one rein, we must take away the contact of that rein [and use the leg on that side near the girth instead] because if you pull, he will continue to pull.

Two students are having difficulties starting their horse in right canter on the left rein [depart in counter-canter].

Technique for the first one:

Renvers [haunches-out to the right] in walk at the wall [tracking left] on the long side and then on a circle [left]. Already place the left leg a little bit back so as not to surprise the horse. When returning to the wall

---

103   [In this case, the action on the right rein must be light and intermittent and the rider must pay attention not to advance the left hand, so as not to lose the left bend. An excessive action on the right rein would send the quarters to the left in a left half-pass position. Therein lies the limit of this action]

104   [With the wrist coming up and maybe with the action of the left leg at the girth (Nuno's advice: replace the action of the hand by the action of the leg on the same side)]

104

[after the circle left], reduce the angle of the travers a little bit and ask for the counter-canter with a light pressure of the left leg, and not by a touch.[105]

Technique for the second one:

It can be useful to first perform the left counter-shoulder-in [shoulder-out] while going right, (this facilitates the right canter depart). Then track left, [continuing with the left counter-shoulder-in through the turn], left leg near the girth, no spur [ending up in a slight shoulder-in left going on the left rein]. Place the whip on the left, possibly on the shoulder, without tapping. Ask for the counter-canter (right lead) on the long side. Left rein to the left [open rein] to place the shoulders (and not the haunches) to the left. All of this without using force. Don't grab. Eventually use a small vibration of the left rein [to dissipate any resistance on the left contact]. It is important to prevent the horse from running. Therefore, short canter without speed.

The left leg must give a light touch on each stride. It is therefore the left leg and the left rein that are acting. These are the *lateral effects.* The rider will pass the corner in a slight left shoulder-in. It is also useful for the rider to accompany the shoulder-in by turning his head to the inside of the arena. [This is the counter-canter position of the young horse with the bend on the side of the turn and not on the side of the lead: right lead, left bend, left shoulder-in position left turn].

Eventually, *cut the counter-canter in small sections.* After a few strides, halt the horse by the left rein. Walk again along the wall in a slight shoulder-in. Start again in counter-canter and do a few more strides of counter-canter each time before a new halt. This technique bites [*mordre*] a little more each time at the short side.[106]

If instead of asking for counter-canter on the long side, we start the true canter on the right rein and then take the diagonal, we must yet again avoid that the horse goes faster and make sure that he reaches the long side well before he reaches the first corner, so he will not be surprised by the corner. Aim well to the exact place you want to reach.

The entire body of the horse must reach the wall, and not just the shoulders.

Keep the horse really close to the wall on the short side, because if he goes away from it, he will fall on the left shoulder.[107]

---

105   [Leg placed a little back. This is the counter-canter position of the trained horse: with the bend on the side of the lead and not the side of the turn, right lead, right bend, slight right travers position, left turn]

106   [This is the progressive method for a horse that cannot yet do the entire short side in counter-canter at once and tends to change leg in front]

107   [This is the method for a horse that has enough balance and flexibility

Canter - the "passade," preparation to the pirouette.[108]

Pass through the [first] corner in counter-canter and go away from the wall by the length of the horse, without using the hand, only an action of the legs to activate and lower the haunches. Then the horse pivots [toward the wall in the second corner] on his inside hind leg [inside hind of the lead of canter] and you only act with your outside leg. The old school used this movement a lot to sit the horse down.

A classical lesson to confirm the collection in the canter.

1) First, circle in walk. Shoulder-in [on another circle]. Tight volte around the haunches [quarters-in]. Choose the right moment to depart into canter, with a very light inside rein.

2) Halt

3) At the halt, pinch lightly with the spur and reinback

4) Depart into canter   i) from the walk
                              ii) from the halt and
                              iii) from the reinback (without a single step of walk).

5) Halt. Reinback and depart to be repeated often.

6) Take the center line from the short side and half-pass.

7) Counter-canter

8) At the beginning of the long side, departs in different places.

9) Hold the outside rein [to sit the horse down] and play with the inside rein [to maintain lightness].

Example of a lesson for a horse that is too excited at the canter.

1) After the transitions walk – trot – halt – shoulder-in on the circle:

2) Departs into canter on the circle

3) Come back to the shoulder-in at the walk and *effet d'ensemble.*

4) In the canter, divide the arena in three big circles. [Turn on those 3 circles one after the other].

5) If the horse is still excited, come back to the classical work at the walk. [Circles, shoulder-in, half-pass, halts].

6) Cease the canter either by a halt with the *effet d'ensemble,* or go

---

to do the entire short side in counter-canter at once. Usually, the rider returns to true canter by taking the diagonal after the passage of the second corner. Nuno Oliveira recommends to adjust the depth of the corner to the balance of the horse and the speed of the canter used to do the counter-canter turns]

108   [The "passade" is an ancient movement in which the horse does two half-turns in succession along the wall separated by a single change. The turn can be done away from the wall or into the wall. In this case, Nuno Oliveira chooses to turn into the wall and uses the corner to frame the movement even more]

back to the walk by abandoning the reins.[109]

Example of another lesson at the canter:
Pass the corner in shoulder-in [in walk] and turn on the center line, being very careful to keep the horse straight on that line. This is the moment to ask the horse to halt. Here, even more than in other exercises, we must remain attentive to the relaxation of the waist, in order to be able to halt without blocking with the hand. When the horse will be confirmed in the halts, we will ask him for two or three steps of reinback and after two or three steps forward in the walk, depart into canter.

Later, when the horse becomes easy and stays calm in this exercise, depart straight from the reinback to the canter. Now, you need the aids to be very light and very accurate, in particular that the hand remains extremely light so that the horse stays calm and straight.

After this preparation, it is time to ask the horse for two new exercises:
1) The canter shoulder-in.
2) The travers in canter and the big circles in half-pass with quarters-in

The correct apprenticeship of the shoulder-in is at the walk first and then in trot which will prepare the horse and create the conditions to start the canter shoulder-in with ease. Increase the number of strides [of canter shoulder-in] very progressively [and start with a very small angle].

Don't forget that, in the same way as in the walk and trot shoulder-in, the inside leg acts near the girth and the outside leg a smidgen further back.

The lightness of the hand (in fact both hands [acting as one]) is a considerable help: can move to the outside and return imperceptibly and delicately to the inside. When the horse will be able to do the entire long side in canter shoulder-in, then go through the corner [in shoulder-in], take the center line still in shoulder-in and from that movement, transition to a canter half-pass back toward the wall [arriving at the middle of the long side].

For the travers [haunches-in] in canter, begin also at the beginning of the long side after passing the [second] corner in shoulder-in position.

The travers can also be continued on the center line: from the shoulder-in [on the short side], transition to the half-pass along the center line.

---

109   [If the horse is not ready (collected enough) to accept the *effet d'ensemble*]

Later, halt the horse in the position of the travers in canter – then reinback and start again in canter.[110]

Canter: It is advantageous to depart in canter from a shorter walk rather than a longer one. This is because in the shorter walk, the horse is rounder and in the longer walk he is more open.

In the canter, if your reins float, there is not accuracy of contact.

Depart into canter from the walk: when you feel that the horse separates the four beats of the walk: 1—2 –3 – 4 (count them in your mind), this is the moment to ask for the canter depart. Therefore, a good depart into canter is the one that results from a good walk, a walk in which the horse is in the hand.

It is the outside rein that maintains the collection in canter.

Don't forget that in canter:

1) The inside rein lowers the head of the horse [by acting down and sideways].

2) The outside rein sits the horse down [by acting upward with the rider's shoulder coming back].

In canter, if we relax the waist sufficiently, we end up moving less with the torso.

In canter, try to see if the horse jumps through and settles in his stride.

If we grip with the legs in the canter, we will bounce in the saddle.

In canter, if we place the horse's head too much to the inside, we throw the shoulders to the outside and the haunches to the inside. And, as the horse becomes wider in the hind-end than in the front, he becomes crooked. He is braced to the inside.

In canter, the torso of the rider must not move anymore than the bascule of the horse. If the rider moves more or less [than the horse's bascule], he opposes [the movement of the horse]. The rider must move with the bascule, not against it, and he needs to relax the waist to achieve [this level of harmony in the canter].

If you depart in canter from an ample walk, you will achieve an ample canter. If you want a canter that is short and collected, depart from a walk that is short and slow.

In canter, it is the calf that must act rather than the spur, to avoid locking the horse's back.

In canter, it is the tailbone of the rider that must go forward, not

110   [In travers position or straight ahead, depending on the level of agility of the horse. This exercise considerably helps the development of balance in the canter and the agility of the horse.]

the loins.[111]

Transitions from canter to walk must be done without the horse raising his head. To achieve this, it is necessary to have:

1) Adjusted reins
2) Not hard hands [soft]
3) Slow down by using the waist.

The transition from canter to walk is even more important than the transition from walk to canter. The return to walk must be done in complete calm without the horse becoming open [losing his collection]. Pay attention to return to walk with the horse balanced on his haunches, not on his shoulders.

In the transitions from canter to walk, try to avoid doing any intermediate trot strides, because trot strides put weight on the shoulders.

We cannot have a light hand at the canter if there is no impulsion and if the rider's torso is not in a good position.

In canter, when we have more inside rein than outside rein, the horses are always crooked and braced.

To a rider: "it is not by pulling on the inside rein that we can slow a horse that pulls at the canter, but it is, for example, by bringing the outside shoulder back, the elbow resting on the hip. In short, we must support [rebalance the horse] by using the outside rein.

A rider that takes too long to prepare a canter depart is a mediocre rider.

In a right circle in canter, "wrap" [the left shoulder and neck with] your left rein, so the horse won't fall on the left shoulder.

We maintain the canter with the outside leg, the other leg works "like a wall" [but without pressing].

The role of the inside leg in canter: it is the outside leg that pushes, but the inside leg is a wall that the horse must never force through. This is particularly important with Iberian horses which are very mobile laterally. But it is an elastic wall rather than a concrete wall. This comment on the role of the inside leg is particularly useful when we start the flying changes.

When the horse has a tendency to rush the canter, don't canter for long periods at a time. Come back gently to walk, without any "jerkiness." Calm him down in the walk and collect him again.

Canter often but for short periods.

When the horse has not yet achieved a sufficient degree of fixity [of the front end] and collection, we return to walk by abandoning [the

---

111   [which might make the shoulders lean forward and "pump" with the bascule]

reins] and not by an action of the reins.

We depart into canter from a walk that is short and slow, with the weight on the hind-end. If the walk is fast, the horse may be able to begin the canter with the head in place [*ramener*], but his hind legs will not be engaged.

In a canter circle, control the circle by the outside leg and not by the reins.

To a rider in canter: "the more you lean forward in canter, the less you control your canter."

After an extension in canter, to reduce [the canter back to a collected gait], you need to push [with the waist].

For the depart in canter from the reinback, the horse must remain sitting and there must be no halt period between the reinback and the depart.

The walk has a lot more to do with the canter than the trot does. In walk, we can prepare the shape of the canter by certain exercises; it is in walk that we prepare the canter.

In canter, the outside leg pushes. The inside leg frames the horse. It is a wall, therefore it stays quiet.

If we do canter departs with a crooked horse, there will be difficulties with the flying changes.

In the "figure eight" in canter, we must keep the same canter during the execution of the entire figure.

With a *young* horse, we perform counter-canter in the bend opposite to the lead. With a *trained* horse, we keep the bend of the canter.

In the counter-canter, the reins only control the speed. If the horse is not confirmed in his collected canter, only perform counter-canter on the short side of the arena.

If in the canter, instead of a regular circle we do a "potato" (sic), the horse can put his weight wherever he wants, on the left or on the right.

If in [true] canter on the left lead, the horse doesn't go to the wall, it is because he has a tendency to fall on the left shoulder. Bring him back to the wall by using the left rein moving toward the right.

In canter circles, don't let your buttocks slide to the outside [of the saddle].

It is out of the question to depart into canter with floating reins [not adjusted properly].

In the circle in canter, don't have any more tension in the inside rein than the outside rein. If we place the head too much to the inside, the haunches also come too much to the inside and the horse is braced on the inside [in a stiff bend]. He is not straight. As needed, bring the shoulders in front of the quarters with the outside rein.

Canter pirouette: We must respect the "rule book" [of the FEI], enter the pirouette in a certain canter, perform it and exit in the same canter.[112]

A horse cannot be correctly connected if the outside rein is "floating" [not correctly adjusted].

1) The inside rein produces the bend and lowers [the position of the head]

2) The outside rein "seats" the horse.

When a horse cantering on the left lead falls on the left shoulder, put him in counter shoulder–in on the right rein [work in the inverted bend for a moment]. Return later to the normal canter by picking up the left rein.

This is an application of the rule: "place the weight where it is needed" [by opposing the quarters to the shoulders].

Canter depart: place the horse in the position of canter depart and get into canter immediately. Don't fiddle [for too long]. It is the uneducated rider who fiddles [before the canter depart].

In canter, we cannot have a light hand if there is not enough impulsion and if the rider's torso is not in place.

Flying changes.
For the flying change, do as little as possible. What is needed is to perfect the first canter [before asking for the change].

When doing flying changes in canter, pay attention that the horse doesn't modify his cadence [neither before nor after the change].

For the flying change from right to left, it is useful to slide the right buttock obliquely to the left, a movement that corresponds to the slight backing of the right shoulder.

It is important that the changes are performed in the calm and relaxed spirit of the canter; we shouldn't hear an "OOMPH" of effort!

Don't let the horse run after a flying change.

When you do a flying change on the long side, don't let the horse stick to the wall.

We need to maintain the same canter, before, during and after the flying change.

When we are cantering in preparation for flying changes, we must be sure that the horse is not crooked, therefore we must maintain a very

---

112   [Even though the pirouettes will be in a 4 beat rhythm while the canter on the straight is in a 3 beat rhythm]

straight neck [no bend].

For the flying changes to be good, it is necessary for the horse to have a good "jump" in the canter. We must feel that there is a sufficient bascule, because it is the form of the canter that matters.

The half-pass in canter sits the horse down and rounds him up, therefore it prepares the flying change.

It is better to do two good flying changes rather than thirty mediocre ones.

One of the secrets of good changes is to keep the shoulders in the same axis as the haunches. However, many riders approach them with the haunches-in.

For the flying change, what matters is not the intensity of the demand that matters but the form of the canter.

Advice for flying changes:

Before:

1) Cadence the canter (for instance use the canter half-pass that increases the collection)

2) Make sure the neck is not crooked but really straight

During:

1) Avoid the canter becoming quick and open (uncollected)

2) Remember: the transition canter - walk is more important that the transition walk – canter. The return to the walk must be done calmly, without the horse exhaling a whisper of contraction and without becoming open or rushed. When the horse can do transitions walk – canter – walk with calm at every place in the arena on either lead, then he is ready to begin the flying changes.

Recommended technique with a horse that begins the flying change.

1) Verify the level of impulsion [to be sufficient].

2) During the last few strides before asking for the change, it is useful to confirm the aids of the lead in which the horse is cantering. [Apply the aids for an instant].

3) Reduce the speed of the canter one or two strides before making the demand to sit the horse down.

4) After the confirmation of the first canter, do the demand (more or less strongly, according to the horse [sensitivity]) by inverting the aids and using a "touch" (electric spur) and not a pressure of the leg.

If you want your horse to remain very flexible laterally, do not place your [outside] leg too far back in the demand for flying changes:

1) First because it is a loss of time, an obstacle to the promptness of the demand;

2) And also because it creates the risk of swinging the haunches

112

(crooked changes).[113]

Before a flying change, survey 1) the level of collection, 2) the speed [of the canter], 3) the cadence. We must prevent the horse from rushing or opening [his frame].

To learn to [do changes without the support] of the wall, ask for the flying change at X on the diagonal or on the center line.

The flying change is not something difficult. What is important is to prepare the correct canter to obtain the change.

If the horse has a tendency to anticipate the flying change (meaning to do it before being asked), we need to confirm the aids of the first canter before the demand, and pay attention that the neck should be straight and not crooked.

When a horse gets excited during the flying changes, after the change ask for a transition to walk by using the torso. Also intersperse some calm halts between the walk and the canter.

For the flying change at X on the diagonal, we must be careful that after passing the second corner to start the diagonal, the outside rein must have the same degree of tension as the inside rein.

Before the flying changes, be careful not to lose contact on the outside rein.

Many riders believe that the horse should be bent in the direction in which the change will be asked. It is a mistake, the neck must be straight.

Do not ask flying changes of a young horse before he is confirmed in counter-canter.

If you do two changes on the long side, the first from true canter to counter-canter and the second from counter to true canter, pay attention that the horse doesn't stick to the wall, particularly in the second change.

For the study of the tempi changes, it is useful at the beginning to count aloud or have somebody with a good sense of the cadence of the canter count aloud: 1-2-3-4//1-2-3-4//1-2-3-4//1-2-3-4

Summary of the technique I recommend with a horse that is starting the flying changes:

1) Verify the impulsion;

2) During the last strides before the change, confirm [slightly reinforce] the aids for the current canter;

3) Eventually, reduce the canter one or two strides before the demand in order to sit the horse (do a half-halt);

4) And then do the demand - more or less strong depending on the horse's [sensitivity] – by inverting the aids, by using an electric touch and

---

113   [and makes the horse contracted in the haunches]

not a pressure of the leg.

For the technique of the flying change from true canter to counter-canter at the beginning of the long side, see the book "Classical Principles of the Art of Training Horses" [*Principes Classique de l'Art de Dresser les Chevaux* now contained in *Oeuvres Complètes* by Nuno Oliveira, Belin 2006].

We must never ask for a flying change in a moment when we are not completely in control of the speed and the cadence. First we must have a well-regulated canter.

To do a flying change, what matters is not so much the intensity of the demand, but rather the impulsion of the first canter.

When we do several changes on the long side (two or three), we must control the canter between the changes, it must not be altered.

For the changes with a trained horse, ask for the changes only with the legs and don't change the position of the reins. The hands only maintain the position of the head and the speed of the gait [on the trained horse].

A greater impulsion in the canter permits the use of less strong aids for the demand of the flying changes.

When we perform tempi changes, we must never alter the neither cadence nor the contact. It is imperative that the reins not move or float.

In the flying changes, the reins are there to place the head, to maintain the neck straight, to slow him down if he rushes, but for nothing else. And don't move your torso.

The degree of collection necessary increases as the changes becomes closer and closer.

We must ask for flying changes when the weight is on the hind-end.

When the horse can do the transitions walk – canter, and canter – walk on either lead in any place in the arena, he is ready for the flying changes. In the changes, not unlike for the canter departs, the rider must not fiddle [with the aids].

If we ask for the changes in a canter without impulsion, they won't be any good.

One of the secrets of the changes consists of confirming the aids of the canter in which we are cantering, until the moment of the change.

If after a first flying change, you let the speed increase and loose the cadence, the horse loses his balance and the second change is less good.

When we diminish the number of strides between each change,

we must prepare by increasing the energy of the canter.

We must not ask for flying changes until the departs into both true and counter-canter from the walk are well-established, and the horse returns to walk without intermediate trot strides. This is because in this case, the horse runs forward while getting on the forehand.

We do not change lead with [the actions of] the hands. The hands are only there to control the speed and the position.

The horse must not accelerate neither before nor after the change. Sometimes we must even slow down a little before demanding it.

In tempi changes, it is useful to look and aim at a distant point (preferably high up) right in front of us.

Only ask the flying changes with the legs. The hands only slow down [the horse if he accelerates]. Place the touch where the leg usually hangs, which is close to the girth. If you use the leg further back,

1) you will contract the haunch and

2) there will be a price to pay when you will ask for the tempi changes.

The secret of tempi changes is:

1) Straightness first

2) Maximum of energy in the right cadence [*rythme*].

There are horses with which we need to shorten the canter for the flying changes and others not. There is no fixed rule. [Some need more canter, others less].

At the moment of a flying change, the horse cannot be on a single rein. He must [have contact] on both reins.

When we do a change, the hands must stay in their place to support the horse and the arms must not creep forward, which would put weight forward [and put the horse on the forehand].

A flying change, if it is asked correctly and not forced, improves the horse's balance.

For flying changes, most riders have a tendency to touch more strongly than needed.

When the horses are travelling too close to the wall, the changes from counter-canter to true canter [and the reverse] are always difficult.

When asking for changes, the hands must stay in their place. If they move forward, the horse escapes, he becomes open, he leans over the front end and puts weight on the forehand.

In the flying changes, the hands' role is to control the tempo and the position, no more than that.

In the flying changes, the riders have the tendency to turn towards the side of the change. It is necessary to do the opposite and bring back the shoulder on the other side of the change [change to the left, bring the right shoulder back].

A flying change "like a rabbit" [a little hop] is a correct change, but in which the horse loses the bascule of the canter. Therefore we need the horse to stay elevated in front without falling on the forehand, at the same time that we try to maintain the horse free of contractions.

If we do canter departs with a crooked horse, we will have difficulties with the changes.

To calm a horse that gets excited with the changes, we must ask him to do them in places and in moments he is not expecting them.[114]

If a horse has a tendency to be late with the hind in changes from counter-canter to true canter, use a round pen if the facility has one. It is useful to begin the changes on the "round." It helps the horse to adjust.[115]

If we are doing changes from counter-canter to true canter with a horse that becomes nervous, do many circles in counter-canter so the horse doesn't know when you will ask for the change, and he is more likely to stay calm.

Progression for the demands of flying changes:

1) First ask for the changes along the wall, from true canter to counter-canter and then from counter-canter to true canter, at any place along the wall.

2) Then ask for the changes on a big circle.

3) Then ask at X on the diagonal.

4) Then we can start to count [for the tempi changes], first along the wall and afterwards, on the diagonal.

It is important that the horse doesn't turn his head in the direction in which he is changing leg.

When we do tempi changes, we must maintain the energy of the canter [between the changes] with the leg that has asked for the change.

With a horse that has difficulties with the changes (a horse who is not a champion that would do changes with any aids), we must place him in the position that is the most helpful for the change and also use a shortened canter. Later, we can advise [on how to improve further].

Something very important is that the horse keep the same canter after the change.

Necessary conditions for [obtaining] (good) changes: we need to have rapid, instantaneous departs, and with a horse that doesn't get crooked.

The secret of the changes is not to use a strong aid, but it is to ar-

114   [instead of at X]
115   [his balance. Changes from true canter to counter-canter on a circle also help a horse that tends to be late behind to "unite" the change.]

rive at the place of the change with energy.

It is important that after a change at X on the diagonal, the horse remain on the same line of the diagonal.[116]

Flying changes: at the beginning with certain horses, we must extend the canter and with others we need to reduce it.

The secret of the flying change is the control of the cadence, of the rhythm and the preoccupation of having the horse with an equal [connection] on both reins, not more on one than the other.

If for the demand, we bring the [outside] leg too far back:

1) The horse will have a tendency to crouch too much or swing the croup,

2) It is also a loss of time in the demand, particularly when we attempt the tempi changes.

For a good change, the horse needs to keep his weight on the hind-end and not become open [lose collection].

In the flying changes, the horse must keep the bascule of the canter. Otherwise, we get changes that are low to the ground, "like a rabbit."

The technique of the first change from true canter to counter-canter along the wall is explained in the book "Classic Principles of the Art of Training Horses," *Principes Classiques de l'Art de Dresser le Chevaux* now contained in *Oeuvres Complètes* by Nuno Oliveira, Belin 2006].

A horse is not ready to do flying changes if:

1) He is not able to do departs to true or counter-canter at any place in the arena.

2) He is not able to do the transition from canter to walk without an intermediate trot stride.

It is important that the horse be well on the hand at the moment of the change [equal contact on both reins]; the eventual quality of the changes depends on the correctness of the canter departs.

Recommendation for the changes with a horse who begins the changes or has a tendency of being late behind:

1) It will be useful to round the horse's [top line] (by using exercises on the haunches for instance).

2) We will need to sustain the energy of the first canter and eventually slow down the speed (half-halt as if you want to halt before the demand for the change).

---

116   [Many horses tend to lose their line and fall on one shoulder after the change]

3) In a change from the left to right, don't let him place his nose to the right nor let him open [his frame].

4) Don't throw the arms forward when you ask for the change, they must stay in place.

5) Make sure the horse is on the hand when you ask for the change!

6) Also use the aid of the whip on the left hip [when asking for a change to the right], if needed.

7) If the demand is done by the spur, it must touch where the leg is [placed naturally], not too far back.

Progression for the one-tempi changes:

1) Don't rush through the steps [be methodical with the progression of the tempi]

2) Before trying them, do isolated changes, then four tempi, then three, then two-tempi.

3) Don't try [the one-tempi] until the other sequences are perfectly known and can be done where and when we want, including on the short sides and on circles.

4) And again, before getting to the one-tempi, be able to return to the two, the three and four tempi.

5) And always finish the lesson by [a session] of two-tempi.

When a horse studies the one-tempi[117], you must finish on that note so he can memorize [the new idea]. But when he knows how to do four [one-tempi] changes (*tac-tac-tac-tac*) [one-one-one-one], return to a line of two-tempi to finish the lesson.

When we start to count the tempi, don't start at four-tempi, but at six or even eight, and then decrease the count between strides gradually: 6-5-4.

---

117   [and does two one-tempi changes starting from each lead for the first time]

118

Chapter 7

HALTS AND REINBACK

The preliminary condition for a good halt is that horse must be well-collected.

To teach the reinback, at the beginning explain the movement to the horse by simple means, from the ground for example.[118]

The preliminary condition of a good reinback is the straight horse. The horse doesn't need to pass through the halt or the immobility [before starting to move backward]. [The reinback] is a movement: it is a swinging from front to back. First increase the impulsion (as done for the halt), then stop the forward movement. Then by the weight and the legs, indicate the rearward direction.

If the horse becomes crooked and you prod him with the spur, it will halt in rigidity. We must do our best to halt the horse by the [action of the] torso. He must halt straight, in peace, without resistance, from back to front, being "in hand" and not open. At the halt, we must not let the head raise. The horse must start again without becoming crooked and without the head lifting, with regular walk steps.

We must halt [the horse] from back to front. Before halting, verify if the horse is quiet and in good impulsion. Therefore, to halt [correctly], we must push. The principle is to send the croup toward the head [by engaging the hind legs], and not to halt by the forehand.

Reinback: When the impulsion is sufficient for the halt, the reinback will happen by itself. If you halt the horse in lightness, he is ready to reinback, don't pull on the reins; no need for it.[119]

The forward push after the reinback must be quicker than the pace of the reinback [which must be slow and deliberate]. He must "leap" forward.

Halt – Reinback

The correct reinback is the consequence of the impulsion of the correct halt. And for a correct halt, we must push [with the waist] to halt the horse, and we must carry on pushing for the horse to go backward. Halt as much as possible with the waist and not by the hands. Therefore, first use the waist to engage [the horse], then the hands that don't move

118   [tapping lightly the front feet in rhythm with the steps with the whip as already explained in a previous chapter]
119   [meaning don't pull with your arms]

n] but follow the torso. Therefore the reins must be adjusted
ack precision.

works for the halt from the trot as well as from the walk.

... ɯ good halt, it is the hind legs which immobilize after the front
legs.

The reinback is useful, but the horse needs to be straight first. We must therefore first halt him straight.

The reinback serves the purpose of having the horse on the hind-end, to put weight back.

If the first step of the reinback is forced, with the horse leaning [on the hand] the following steps will be rushed. So, at the same time that we use the torso to push, lift the hands before the halt, and if need be, do a little vibration before the reinback.

A reinback serves to have the horse on the hind-end. We flow back [*on fait refluer le poids*] the weight towards the hind-end.

We must prepare the halt. Therefore before halting, we must push. We halt by [using our] back with the least amount of rein possible.

Before the halt, the walk must be slow. The halt is asked by the torso. The fingers close and open immediately after the halt is obtained. The horse must not lower is head and dive down. He must keep the same head position and the same contact.

For the halt with *l'effet d'ensemble* [comprehensive effect], the legs act first and the hands [immediately] afterwards.

A horse is not truly forward when he is not easy in his reinback. He must swing [back and forth] easily.

Halt

1) First the legs, so push [delicately]. Eventually use the *effet d'ensemble.*

2) Close the fingers, fix the hand.

3) Grow the rider's torso. The poll must stay in place, the mouth soft, with a direct flexion.

The rule is that the horse keeps his impulsion in the halt. In this condition, he is as ready to go backwards as to go forward. He is halted on the haunches. He holds his posture.

Halt [at any time] *during training:* to halt in any gait, we must start by using comprehensive actions to noticeably increase the impulsion.

When we do reinbacks of six or seven steps several times in a row, we must intersperse a few reinbacks of only one or two steps and push forward immediately. So the horse doesn't start to believe that he will always go back six or seven steps![120]

When the horse has a sufficient impulsion for the halt, the reinback happens by itself. If you halt the horse in lightness, he is ready to reinback.

Reinback: don't ask for it when the weight is on the forehand, so obtain lightness first.

To halt, we push and don't pull on the reins, but we oppose the waist [which means] that we prepare the halt by [increasing] impulsion.

For a horse that becomes contracted in the reinback and rushes by blocking his haunches [when the hind legs get stuck under the body and do not step back properly well behind the croup]: do very small circles the size of the length of horse's body at the walk in shoulder-in, and (we are tracking right rein) on the right snaffle rein; and when you feel that there is no longer a resistance on the right rein and the horse is calm, [place the horse] along the wall and ask for only one or two steps of reinback, then go forward immediately.

[This exercise] allows us to unblock the horse's haunches in preparation for reinback.

The reinback of an *untrained horse* is [frequently] in four beat, just like the walk which is in four beat.

The reinback of a *trained* horse is in two beat by diagonalization.

And the horse must advance the hind leg that is back in order to halt square.

Reinback: we do not reinback by the reins, that would be acting on the front end. If we start by the reins, we pull the mouth backward, but the hind legs end up dragging.

We must act first on the haunches – touch of the spurs if necessary to activate the hind legs – and we oppose with the hand afterwards.

The reinback is a useful exercise, in a condition that it is calm and straight, and that at the moment of the depart forward, the shoulders don't waver left or right.

Before a halt, we must put the horse "on the ball," otherwise his hind legs will be far behind, and he will have to make an effort to reinback and he will rush. The reinback will be too quick. The reinback must be slower than the depart forward.

120   [Nuno Oliveira includes the forward movement that follows the reinback in the actual reinback concept, a little bit like what the Germans call the *Shaukel*: several sequences of counted forward and backward steps]

It is useful during the exercises to do many halts, but we must halt in such a way that the front legs stop before the hind legs [the hind legs do the final step forward in order to engage under the body]. Therefore, use the torso before the hand. Briefly, we need a halt full of impulsion. It is the front legs that halt first.

Advice: don't halt [when the horse is] in resistance.

The lateral movements give impulsion and flexibility, however don't forget to frequently ride the center line [on single track].

Don't start a reinback without first having the feeling that the horse is "well in front of you" [in front of the aids].

Chapter 8

THE SHOULDER-IN:
KEY EXERCISE OF DRESSAGE

The shoulder-in is an exercise that relaxes, supples and engages horses.

When you start the shoulder-in, turn your nails of the inside rein upwards and direct this hand toward your outside shoulder (in such a way that if the rein got longer, you would actually touch that shoulder).

In the shoulder-in, we need:
1) to feel that the horse is in self-carriage,
2) receive on the outside rein the action of the inside rein,
3) help [the movement] with the seat as follows: get the weight to pass alternately from the inside buttock to the outside buttock, in the direction of the movement.[121]
4) Feel the weight on the inside hind leg and not on the outside shoulder.

In an attempt at shoulder-in with a young horse, if he resists, don't insist. Do a small circle before restarting the shoulder-in. Sometimes, also halt in the position of the shoulder-in and start again afterwards.

The shoulder-in loses some of its usefulness if the rider doesn't obtain a degree of lightness superior to the one he had when he started. In short, the horse [must] become lighter as he executes [the shoulder-in].

In the shoulder-in, if the horse releases [yields to the aids] and you carry on acting with the inside leg, you will rush the gait.

Before starting the shoulder-in, put the horse in the kind of walk in which he will have to execute the shoulder-in.

In the shoulder-in, the horse must be relaxed, otherwise [the exercise] has no value. The horse must be slightly bent around the inside leg but without excess. We must feel that both shoulders are "inside" the track, not just one, and we must not feel that the weight is falling on the outside shoulder.

Try to do your shoulder-in with very little pressure of the inside leg, so the horse can relax.

---

121   [Follow the swing of the back created by the lateral action of the hind legs]

The shoulder-in is easy if we start it delicately. But if we do too many things at the beginning, the horse will resist.

In the shoulder-in right, we send the horse to the left by using the right rein and the right leg, but we must control with the left rein so the weight doesn't fall to the left.

In a shoulder-in, when we arrive at the end of the long side, the horse must be more supple, more relaxed. If the shoulder-in is poorly done, the horse will end up more rigid.

In the passing of each corner exists a little piece of shoulder-in: in walk, trot and canter. It is true in all three gaits.

The shoulder-in on the diagonal must have less bend than the one along the wall.

In the shoulder-in, the walk must be cadenced and slow, otherwise the horse cannot engage. Because they are concerned about a potential loss of impulsion, many riders demand a walk that is too rapid and too jerky.

The shoulder-in is an exception to the rule that we must engage the hind legs before starting the exercise. Here, it is the exercise that makes the horse engage, not the preparation. [Engagement] is not a precondition, it is a consequence.

When you are in shoulder-in, send your body toward your outside elbow.[122]

In shoulder-in, everything we do with the inside rein must have an effect felt by the outside rein. The [correct] support of the reins prevents the horse from becoming crooked in the neck (which is a sign that he is not forward).

The number of tracks [in the shoulder-in], (two, three or four) is of little importance. Here is what really matters in the shoulder-in:

1) Angle of 30 to 45 degrees, more or less,[123]
2) Equal tension on both reins,
3) Feeling the weight on the inside hind and not on the outside shoulder.

In the shoulder-in, we must feel that the weight must always remain on the inside hind, but also that the outside shoulder stays inside the

---

122   [with the outside rein controlling the movement of the outside shoulder]
123   [According to the needs of each horse and the amplitude of the gait the shoulder-in is performed in. A smaller angle facilitates a bigger gait, more angle suits a more collected gait.]

124

arena and avoids the tendency to return to the wall.[124]

In the shoulder-in, we must feel that the croup is active. We must feel that it is energetic and doesn't drag behind a "broken" neck [crooked]. Same for the counter-shoulder-in, feel that it is the croup that advances and not the neck that is broken [bends too much at the base].

It is said: put the weight in the direction of the movement. More precisely, I would say: the rider needs to accompany [the movement]. In one step, he pushes his buttocks to the outside; in the next step the horse brings him back to the inside; in the next one, the horse takes him to the outside again, and so forth. So the rider goes with the movement and it is the horse that brings him back to the other side.

In the shoulder-in, don't lift the rider's inside shoulder, to the contrary, it is better to relax it. *The hand begins with the shoulder.* In the shoulder-in, use the inside rein to bend without creating rigidity. The wrist of

Antoine in a lesson with the Master, riding Campo, at the Hussière stable of Hélène Arianoff.

---

124   [through the vigilance of the outside rein]

the inside hand must be relaxed.

If you don't begin the shoulder-in the corner and benefit from the position [given by the corner], you will end up having to use a rougher movement to obtain it. This confirms the importance of [using] the original position of the exercise [in the corner], because afterwards, it is harder to regulate [the exercise]. Example: shoulder-in right: if you feel that there is too much weight on the left shoulder, act less with the right rein and further the effects of the left rein and the right leg.

In the shoulder-in, the weight of the horse must be on the inside hind and not on the outside shoulder. The outside hind must not go too wide and go beyond the leg of the rider.

Half-pass and shoulder-in: the goal isn't to force the horse to do the exercise rather to do so with a relaxed horse. It must be the horse that is doing this of his own accord. To be effective, the shoulder-in must not be forced, otherwise the horse will become contracted. In view of the shoulder-in on the circle, we must bring the young horse to bend. We must obtain a supple yielding of the croup, a natural undulation of the croup, but without force.

In the shoulder-in the neck cannot be "broken" [over-bent laterally] and we must feel that the weight is on the inside hind, not the outside shoulder. Support the outside.

In the shoulder-in, send the horse with the inside leg and receive him with the outside leg. The classic authors used to say: "in the balance of the heels."

Each corner of the arena is a little piece of shoulder-in.

We must enter into the shoulder-in without force.

If the shoulder-in is the continuation of the passing of the corner, it is easy, afterwards, we do not need to intervene too much with the aids.

In the shoulder-in, after two or three strides, the outside aids become more important than the inside aids to help maintain a constant angle and speed. [Without them] we throw the weight on the outside shoulder.

The left shoulder-in consists of bringing the left shoulder inside the track, but also the right shoulder to the inside. Both shoulders [need to be brought inward].

If in the shoulder-in, we place the head too much to the inside, we end up throwing the weight on the outside shoulder.

In the shoulder-in, we must control the outside carefully so the weight doesn't fall on that side.

It is useful to begin the shoulder-in (in walk or trot) when the head of the horse arrives at the end of the short side.

Whichever exercise you are doing, you must do it through preparation and not through surprise. For example, we ask for the shoulder-in after the short side because the horse is already bent and the inside leg is already in place, etc.. This is why I say: "marry the circle, the corner and the shoulder-in."

The shoulder-in:

1) In reality, it is the *two* shoulders-in, this is why the outside shoulder must be placed away from the wall and come "inside" [the arena].

2) Before starting it, we must establish the walk in which we want to perform the shoulder-in.

3) And then, start with the inside aids and follow by the outside aids.

The shoulder-in on the center line is useful, but only after the horse can do shoulder-in along the wall without stepping away from it.

In the shoulder-in, don't "carry" the horse with the inside leg.

In the shoulder-in, it is not the inside leg that pushes [the horse sideways]: [if done that way] the haunches would step outward [and lose their engagement].

In the shoulder-in, the outside aids support and regulate. It is the outside rein that is fixed, while in the half-pass, it is the opposite (it is the inside rein that is fixed).

In lateral movements, the horse must perform full strides, not half-strides.[125]

In the circle with shoulder-in, (as in all shoulder-in exercises), we must feel that the whole horse is truly working and not that the hind-end is dragging.

Start the shoulder-in *IN* the corner and not after. The corner facilitates the beginning of the shoulder-in. The circle, the corner and the shoulder-in form a *ménage a trois* [a marriage of three exercises].

In a shoulder-in, the horse must keep the same walk that he had before starting it. In trot after a circle, start the shoulder-in, making sure that the horse doesn't reduce or diminish his trot.

In the shoulder-in with a horse that is learning the exercise, pay more attention to the work of the hind-end than to the bend.

If, in shoulder-in, the horse gets behind the hand, meaning that if the inside rein is floating, it is because the neck is "broken" [over-bent laterally].

---

125   [with the same lateral amplitude as the forward amplitude the horse had in the gait traveling on single track]

We can do shoulder-in a straight line everywhere [in the arena], but if we do it on the long side near the wall, we must insist that the horse does it with the croup near the wall [for the entire execution of the movement]. This helps the rider prevent the horse from "playing accordion" [losing his collection and stretching out] and putting weight on his shoulders.

The shoulder-in loses its usefulness if the horse doesn't become lighter through performing it. The rider should obtain [at the end of the exercise] a degree of lightness superior to the one he had when he started the movement.

In the left shoulder-in, if the horse wants to distance his croup from the wall, the rider must move his left shoulder back to bring the croup back to the wall.

Walk shoulder-in: the horse must keep the same cadence as is needed in a slow walk with four distinct beats. If the croup drags, it is not by bringing the inside leg back that we will remedy it. What is needed is to use the outside aids to bring the outside shoulder more to the inside. The shoulder-in requires that the horse is bent around the inside leg. Therefore the inside leg must be close to the girth [rather than back pushing the croup sideways].

If, in a shoulder-in, the croup doesn't advance enough, don't bring the inside leg back because it will make the quarters fall outwards and the weight will fall on the outside, when it should be on the inside [haunch]. The remedy is to act with the outside leg and the outside rein which bring the shoulders more to the inside track, as well as bring back the [rider's] inside shoulder.

Don't let the horse reduce the walk in the shoulder-in. Do it in the same walk [as the single track walk].

In the shoulder-in, we do not need even an ounce of weight in the reins. The horse must not force or put any weight [in the reins]. [However], make sure the horse doesn't lose the contact of the inside rein and don't omit to support him with the outside rein. Try, however possible, to keep the [surface of the] inside rein in contact with the body [neck] of the horse and not opened [widened].

Shoulder-in left: don't start by pulling on the left rein, (bringing the head to the left) because if the horse turns his head [too much] to the left, he will generally put the weight on the right shoulder. We must therefore start with the right rein bringing the right shoulder off the track and to the inside [of the arena]. [Immediately] after that, start using the left leg. Therefore the first aid is the outside rein that brings the outside shoulder inward.

128

The shoulder-in is nothing more than bending the horse to the inside, sending him to the outside rein.

In the left shoulder-in *on a circle*, the left rein goes to the right and the right rein goes to the right as well. This right rein receives the action of the left rein.

If you start the shoulder-in by pulling the inside rein, you end up being busy throwing weight on the outside.

In a shoulder-in to the right:

1) The outside left rein brings the shoulders to the inside.

2) [Immediately] afterwards, the right shoulder of the rider comes back.

In a shoulder-in on a circle, feel that the haunches advance in the same stride [length as in the single track work] and not by "half strides."

When we pass a corner in walk in shoulder-in, we must support the shoulders a little and make the haunches march a little more. In effect, they have a greater distance to cover[126].

With a very young horse, for the shoulder-in on the long side, we can halt him after the second corner of the short side, put him in position of shoulder-in and begin it from the halt.

The shoulder-in and the half-pass are exercises designed to make the horse supple, to activate and to engage the hind legs so the horse can later walk straight with more activity.

In the shoulder-in, the rider must "receive" the horse with his outside calf.

If during the shoulder-in the rider can proceed [for the rest of the movement] without using his inside leg, it means that the horse has "given" [has released].

In the shoulder-in as well as in the croup to the wall [haunches-out, renvers], the croup must stay close to the wall. Otherwise, the horse opens. The same is true of the "head to the wall" [haunches-in, travers], the [horse's] head should be kept close to the wall.

At the beginning of the shoulder-in [work], it is sometimes useful to change the contact from one rein to the other so the horse doesn't lean on the hand, until the horse learns to do the shoulder-in without any weight on the reins.

In lateral exercises, the horse must make complete strides not "half strides". He must take regular steps, [not short ones]. So during the shoulder-in, the horse must keep the same stride than the one he used when initiating it. Same in the trot, he cannot reduce or diminish his trot.

---

126   [Because the haunches are on a wider arc of travel than the shoulders, when the shoulder-in is performed through the circle.]

The shoulder-in (as well as the half-passes) must be done at the collected walk.

If in a shoulder-in, you feel that the horse puts too much weight on the outside shoulder, act more with the outside aids than with the inside aids.

In the shoulder-in, the horse must be relaxed, otherwise it is without merit. He must be light. He must let go of the bit and not lean on the hand.

The shoulder-in is an exercise to relax, supple and engage horses. If you rush while doing it, these results will elude you.

It is preferable to start the shoulder-in *in* the corner rather than *after* the corner. This facilitates the beginning of the shoulder-in on the long side.

In the shoulder-in with a beginner horse, pay more attention to the work of the hind-end than to the bend.

In shoulder-in, we must feel that the inside of the horse is completely relaxed, that it is flexible. The "fat of the calf" on the inside must act close to the girth, from back to front (by rolling [on the ribs]) and the outside leg [acts] a smidgen further back.

In the shoulder-in: the horse must keep the same contact on both reins. Don't bend the neck too much, because otherwise, the inside rein is no longer in contact; the horse is behind the rein. So the horse must be slightly bent around the inside leg, not too much. The head must not pass beyond the line of the [horse's] inside shoulder.

When in a shoulder-in the horse goes "on his own accord" [in self-carriage], keep the reins in position, but without action; however, they must be ready to intervene in a fraction of a second.

In a shoulder-in with a young horse (more like 1/8th of a shoulder-in), if he starts resisting, don't insist. Do a small circle and restart your light shoulder-in. And occasionally, halt in the position of the shoulder-in and then restart again.

The correct shoulder-in is "the aspirin of dressage." It remedies everything: resistances, lack of impulsion, etc.

In the shoulder-in, the outside hind leg must not go too wide and go beyond the outside leg of the rider. For the bend of the neck, the head must not go beyond the line of the [inside] shoulder.

The shoulder-in is a large corner of the arena that never ends or really prolongs itself to the end of the long side.

The [good] shoulder-in increases the engagement of the hind legs, rounds and supples the horse. A poorly executed shoulder-in serves no purpose. It makes the horse crooked and contracted.

130

Recapitulation of the principle points of the shoulder-in:

1) The preparation is done in the corner.

2) The horse must be bent from head to tail like a banana and not broken at [the base] of the neck to the inside. The head must not pass the line of the [inside] shoulder.

3) Inside leg near the girth [acting from back to front] and the outside leg slightly further back [receiving the horse].

4) Inside rein [acting] in the direction of the rider's outside shoulder. Outside rein parallel to the body of the horse to support[127] and feel with that outside rein everything the inside rein is doing.

5) Besides some particular cases (of some precise exercises) in which the rider's weight must stay on the inside, the weight of the rider must pass alternately from one buttock to the other, from the inside to the outside in the direction of the movement.

6) Feel that both shoulders [of the horse] are to the inside the arena [inside track] and that the horse puts his weight on the inside hind leg and not on the outside shoulder.

---

127   [the balance of the horse]

Chapter 9

HALF-PASS

Technique of the half-pass:

We bend the horse on the short side [of the arena] with the inside aids. So the combined actions of the inside rein and the inside leg give the bend (the leg bends and the rein receives the bend).[128]

In the half-pass, use the outside rein to fix most issues [angle, direction, etc.]. Because, if we use the inside rein, we [automatically] take away from the impulsion. The role of the inside rein is to secure the bend, but if we have too much inside rein, we block the shoulder on the side the horse is half-passing.

In the half-pass, we must feel that the haunches are pushing.

Half-passes (as well as shoulder-ins) must be done in collected walk.

In the half-pass, the [rider's] inside leg is more important than the outside leg.

In the counter changes of hand, in order to keep the symmetry of the degree of obliqueness [angle], it is recommended to do a little forward step [with the horse straight] in between the two half-passes.

In a half-pass (in walk, trot or canter), we must be more concerned with the activity of the haunches than the bend. In the half-pass, the horse has a tendency to rush the last two steps before reaching the wall[129]. This is why the rider must be vigilant with the inside leg [all the time].

In the half-pass, if the horse throws his weight on the shoulder on the side to which he is half-passing, it is because he is rushing and not in balance.[130]

The rider has finally understood what is really a half-pass the day he knows that the inside leg is more important than the outside leg. If he doesn't need the outside leg[131], it is because the horse has started the half-pass with enough impulsion.

---

128   [Then the horse is ready to start a half-pass on the diagonal by the use of the outside aids after he passes the second corner]

129   [as well as be lazy in the first two strides when leaving the wall]

130   [This can be corrected by opening and lifting the outside rein slightly, putting less weight on the inside seat bone and by supporting the horse with the inside leg]

131   [and starts the movement with outside rein and inside leg]

If, with a given horse, you have difficulties in the half-pass, don't insist; it is better to return to lateral steps [leg yield without bend] rather than worry about the bend.

The important part of a half-pass at the walk is that the horse does the last two steps of the half- pass in the same cadence [as the rest of the movement].

In the half-pass: we often use the outside leg too soon. Also, when the horse has "given" [entered the half-pass without resistance], cease the use of the outside leg and support [the movement] with the inside leg. It is principally with the inside leg that we support the half-pass. A good half-pass is the one in which the horse reaches the wall more by being supported by the inside leg than by being pushed by the outside leg. It is the proof that the horse had a sufficient impulsion from the beginning.

In summary, the *beginning* of half-pass includes two phases:

Phase 1: start with the inside aids to put the horse in position of shoulder-in.

Phase 2: then use the outside aids to begin the sideways march and advance forward.

During the half-pass: the inside leg supports, helps maintain the impulsion and keeps the bend. The horse must be more supported by the inside leg than pushed by the outside leg.

In the half-pass, the rider must have the sensation that the front "follows" the back, and not that the haunches follow the front end.[132]

If you do a *doubler* [turn on the center line] with lacks of impulsion before the half-pass, there will be a high risk that the half-pass will be bad. The horse will enter the half-pass "open" [without collection].

The quality of a half-pass (in walk or trot) is verified by the perfection of the last step. If the half-pass begins with enough impulsion, it will be based on the support of the inside leg and not the push of the outside leg.

In a half-pass (walk, trot): it is sometimes useful to open the outside rein in the direction opposed to the one we are traveling, in order to increase the lateral movement of the haunches.[133]

We must only start half-passes with young horses when they
_____
132   [The horse is pushed by the haunches, and the haunches are not dragging]
133   [This is a very important concept in Nuno Oliveira's work to use the opening of the outside rein (without inverting the bend created by the inside rein) to control the angle of the haunches]

134

achieve a sufficient degree of impulsion. Until then, lets limit our work to simple lateral steps.

In a walk half-pass, the inside leg
1) receives the horse
2) maintains the bend
3) maintains the cadence.

Again: the aids of the half-pass are more based on the inside leg than inside rein or outside leg.

The last step of half-pass toward the center line already belongs to the straight center line, it is integrated in it. This is why the horse must get there by the use of the inside leg and not by the outside leg that pushes.

To a rider doing a trot half-pass: "get the haunches to work more, and for that, open the outside rein to help the action of the outside leg."

If a horse gets tense in the half-pass [and tends to lose his bend], it is advisable to only do small pieces of half-pass at a time and to return to the shoulder-in (on a small circle for instance) and return to the half-pass with the same [light] bend. For example (walk or trot), do a few steps of shoulder-in along the long side (a few steps *only*), then go into three or four steps of half-pass and return again to the shoulder-in on a circle with the same bend. The idea is to cut the shoulder-in and the half-pass into small pieces, until the horse can do those exercises for longer without tension.[134]

In the travers to the right [haunches-in right], the right leg:
1) Controls the bend,
2) Helps maintain the impulsion.

In a travers [haunches-in] in walk to the right, if the haunch doesn't move enough to the right, we can open the left rein. This reinforces the action of the left leg.

The travers is only useful if it is done with enough angle [30 to 45 degree], otherwise it only teaches the horse to never be straight on the long side.

In the travers, we must support the inside of the bend [by the action of the inside leg].

In the counter-shoulder-in [shoulder-out], we must support the outside[135] [with outside rein and leg], so the weight stays on the inside hind and doesn't fall on the outside shoulder !

---

134   [Another exercise practiced by Nuno Oliveira for horses which lacked forwardness in the half-pass was to do a few steps of half-pass, then a few steps straight on by effect of the inside leg, then return to half-pass in the original direction, then a few straight steps, etc.]

135   [In this case, "outside" is the outside of the bend, not the outside of the arena in shoulder-out/counter shoulder-in]

Canter half-passes:

In a good canter half-pass, the horse jumps to the side. In a bad one, the horse slides to the side.

In a canter half-pass, we must do nothing with the reins. It is the business of both legs.

A canter half-pass does not mean running sideways, but jumping sideways.

If he slides sideways instead of jumping, it is because he is on the forehand.

When you do a *doubler*[136] in canter in preparation for a half-pass, keep the bend with the inside leg but support with the outside aids.

In the canter half-pass, feel that the horse jumps sideways. Each stride of the half-pass must be distinct from the previous one, it is a series of jumps [*bonds*]. Otherwise, he slides sideways and put his weight on the inside shoulder.

It is not with the blows of the spur that we succeed at half-passing.

Only intervene in the half-pass if the horse loses his position. So we can apply the rule by which, when we have placed the horse in position of half-pass and he has started it correctly, we must cease to act. That will be the reward for his obedience. Continuing with the demand [actions of the aids] would likely perturb him. "So, I have obeyed! What else does the rider want?" It is a question of psychology.

Certainly cease the action, but keep the legs close in order to:

1) Be able to intervene quickly,

2) Not surprise the horse with the legs, because if they were far [from the horse's sides] they would only intervene with abruptness.

Half-passing is moving sideways with flexibility, it is not rushing sideways, which would be a way of [a horse] defending himself.

It is necessary for the horse to "meet the hand" on the side of the half-pass.

[With a young horse,] start the walk half-pass (which is different than side steps) [which we may call leg yielding in English], only after the horse performs the shoulder-in in trot correctly [and with ease].

---

136   [Center line]

Chapter 10

PIAFFE, PASSAGE, SPANISH WALK

In piaffe, the horse must as relaxed in his head [mind] as he is in the walk.

He must be able to stay in [the piaffe], without groaning or tensing his mouth.

We must not force the horse to piaffe, but create the desire to get into piaffe.

The walk that precedes the piaffe must already contain the piaffe. We cannot piaffe with a horse who is heavy in front. And the more we compress the horse, the less he will piaffe.

The piaffe must not be a manifestation of excitement, but to the contrary, be used to calm and dominate.

In piaffe, the spurs contract the horse.

The piaffe is not only a "presentation air," but a degree of *moral and physical collection* [*rassembler*].

The majority of riders cannot piaffe because, earlier in the training, when they were practicing the preparatory lateral movements and using the so-called "collected walk," they were using a walk that is too ample[137].

As long as a horse is not confirmed in piaffe, it is a mistake to transition [from piaffe] into a big extended trot under the pretext of sending him forward. [That doesn't work because] it puts the horse in a position contrary to the one needed for the piaffe, in which the horse must be round.

From a true piaffe, we can depart into any gait: reinback, walk, trot, even canter.

In the beginning, don't demand too much movement. The horse must enter the piaffe with the same calm as in walk. It is only later that we develop the movement.

The piaffe should achieve an improvement in balance and the horse must finish the piaffe by staying round and relaxed, so he can transition into any gait from there. This is not possible if he is tense and nervous.

We prepare the position of piaffe in the exercise that precedes it

---

137   [too extended instead of really short and cadenced, which is what is really needed to achieve a truly relaxed and collected piaffe]

and we enter piaffe with light aids.

The walk that precedes it must contain the piaffe. The horse must enter the piaffe calmly and exit it calmly also.

In the study of piaffe, we need the horse to mobilize in the relaxation [start moving his diagonal pairs in place].

Piaffe: if necessary [to create impulsion], touch the horse [with the spur or the whip] *before* to put him "on the ball." When he enters the piaffe, leave him in peace. So prepare and let him do it. What is needed, is that the horse enters the piaffe with ease.

When a horse has a tendency to stick his front feet forward in the piaffe, don't ask for piaffe in place, but go slightly forward at each step.

If at the beginning of piaffe, the horse crosses his [front] legs or balances [widens his hind legs], don't worry about cadence: go faster and advance more.

Nuno Oliveira makes a distinction between the piaffe in which the horse increases his balance, which is useful [sits down more], and the forced piaffe in which the horse "opens" himself [hollows out] and stiffens his back.

It is indispensable that the rider knows exactly when to start the apprenticeship of the piaffe. With certain horses, it is useful to start the piaffe in-hand early in the training. Asking the piaffe under saddle too soon can be a major mistake for the entire life of the horse.

From the beginning of the piaffe training, the horse must be completely straight.

In the piaffe training, we must stop often and let the horse return to calm and stretch his neck.

In the execution of the piaffe, don't forget the principle: "position and let [him] do" [*placer et laisser faire*].

One of the most important things in the tact of a trainer is to know exactly what dose of relaxation and nervous influx we need to execute such and such exercise. For the piaffe, we have a tendency to call for too much nervous influx; as a consequence, each time we ask for piaffe, the horse gets a little excited.

We need to be well aware of the strength of the horse's hocks to know to which degree we can ask the horse to sit in his piaffe.

We don't piaffe with low hands.

The more the legs are loose, the better the horse piaffes. At the beginning, choose the place [in the arena] where the horse piaffes best.

The piaffe must always be an improvement of balance [*prise d'equilibre*].

The diagonal mobilization becomes piaffe when suspension appears [really cadence].

We must enter the piaffe and exit it in peace.

Piaffe: it is sometimes useful, in order to straighten the horse, to follow Baucher's advice: balance the hands from left to right and right to left.

Piaffe [under saddle]: go along the wall in a very energetic, very short walk. Eventually (but not necessarily), use a little pinch of the spurs, sharp and quick. Right away, ask for the piaffe. Don't dwindle. What counts is the quickness of the mobilization [the rapidity of the response to the aids]. We obtain the piaffe, not by hitting the horse but by keeping him light. The hand must be very light. It is a matter of roundness [of the top line] rather than nerves. The more we hit the horse in the piaffe, the more the horse enters in revolt. At the beginning, don't preoccupy yourself with [too much] slowness in the movement.

Study of the piaffe in-hand from the ground ["work in hand"]:

1) Don't use too much hand, conditional freedom [of the mouth] from the hand.[138]

2) Touch the horse in different places.[139] (Use not strong but electric touches),

3) When we stop, the horse must stay completely immobile.[140]

For the piaffe, the work at the wall from the ground must be done with a lot of tact and delicacy. Before starting it, the horse must know the shoulder-in and the half-pass asked with the whip from the ground.[141]

The aid of the whip is very important. The horse must accept the contact of the whip all over his body, so that he doesn't get scared every time the trainer makes a movement with the arm that holds the whip and that his eye keeps a trusting expression.

In the work in-hand, we need to know for each horse, where to touch on the hind-end, see which position [and which movement] he adopts when he is touched in this or that place.

With long reins: the piaffe work can be very useful to improve im-

---

138   [This means to keep the hand as much as possible in one place to keep the horse in place, but not maintaining a constant contact]

139   [Croup, thighs, flank, hocks, even withers to study the reaction of the horse and find out which location works best, this location may change as training progresses]

140   [Press the whip on the loins (*effet d'ensemble* of the whip) to obtain immobility if needed]

141   [If the horse doesn't know the lateral work from the ground when we start the piaffe, confusion will set in later and the horse will engage instead of going sideways or vice versa]

pulsion and straightness.

Passage

We passage by the legs and not by the hands.

In passage, if a horse has a tendency to go too fast, touch the hind leg with the whip [without tapping him] (on the inside of the arena) at the moment the hind leg is about to lift. It is the whip touching at each step [at the moment of engagement] that reduces [the length of the stride, hence the speed].

To a rider in passage: "don't let the haunches come to the right. Straighten him with the right leg and the left hand."[142]

When we change direction in passage, it is the legs and not the hands that determine the direction. Otherwise, we unbalance the horse.

The beginning of passage is already "passage," in the sense that it is the cadence of the passage in the trot, which is different from the "passage-like trot."

If a horse passages without being collected [light in hand and engaged behind], it is a form of resistance; it is the "passage-like trot."

To a rider: "don't start the study of the passage now. It is too soon. Your horse is not energetic nor collected enough in his canter."

In the passage, the elevation is to be appreciated, but the most important element is the suspension. The true passage is defined by La Guérinière [short, elevated, sitting]. The modern passage is a hovering trot.

In an air of high school, (passage for instance), we must not start by preoccupying ourselves with elevation. When we teach a high school air, we must first create the mechanics. We ask for a bigger movement later. We must not necessarily judge a passage by the height of his movement. Each horse, according to his breed, his conformation, etc. achieves his own height. What matters is the moment of suspension between each diagonal stride.

In passage, use your outside lateral aids to prevent the horse from sticking to the wall.

Transition piaffe-passage:

In the transition from piaffe to passage, lower [descendez] the legs a little to reduce the piaffe a little bit and help the horse pass more easily into passage without jerkiness.

If in passage, the horse puts more weight on one shoulder than

---

142   [By placing the shoulders in front of the haunches with the hand and holding the haunches behind the shoulders with the legs]

the other, balance your hands slightly from right to left and left to right to re-establish the balance.

To improve the *amplitude of the passage,* it is done by [slowing down] the cadence. Often the horse goes to fast. We must slow him down and then touch the horse in cadence[143].

To a rider that accompanies the passage [with exaggerated movement]: "it is the horse that must passage, not the rider."

I ask the first strides of passage with a lower front end, with the purpose of obtaining a good lift from the hind legs. After that I work on the front legs, once the horse is collected.

To go from passage to piaffe, we must reduce the passage by a comprehensive action [*action d'ensemble*] .

To go back from piaffe to passage, open the fingers.

In the passage, there is a time of suspension; in the piaffe, there must also be one, however short it may be.

In piaffe, the lower joints must bend.

In passage: for the left diagonal, touch with the right leg and vice versa.

Spanish Walk and Spanish Trot.

As we will need to touch the horse on the shoulder to ask for the *Spanish trot,* don't put the whip forward for the piaffe nor the passage, so there is no confusion.

For the Spanish trot, place your legs further forward than for the piaffe or the passage.

Spanish walk: don't use your spur for the Spanish walk, only the calf.

Spanish trot: in the true Spanish trot, the horse doesn't throw his foot forward but lifts it upwards.

Spanish walk: give the indication, then do as little as possible. Act with the back and not with the reins. Let him do it. If a front leg lifts less than the other, use the whip on the shoulder rather than the leg.

For the Spanish walk: have the horse straight, hold only by the snaffle, without blocking the horse and without using your spur.

When you ask for the "*jambette*" [lifting of the front leg] of the right front, prevent the horse from leaning on the right rein and vice versa.

---

143   [with a light touch of the spurs in time with each stride]

Chapter 11

THE YOUNG HORSE

When you are choosing a young horse in the view of buying, pay more attention to the quality of the canter rather than the trot, because it is easier to perfect the trot than the canter.

Remember: to teach beginner riders [beginner at training horses] that the notion of obtaining forward movement without using force is a rule that suffers no exception. Read: *Les chevaux et leur cavaliers,* "The horses and their riders," now contained in *Oeuvres Complètes* by Nuno Oliveira, Belin 2006.

I want a horse that is energetic and forward. However, my equitation is based on the physical and mental relaxation [of the horse] and the absence of force [from the rider], because everything done with force tightens and tenses the horse.

Collection is based on relaxation. If it based on compression, it is no longer "collection."[144]

Equitation is very simple. It suffices to respect thousands of little details. It is the execution that is difficult.[145]

Instead of "dressage"[146], we should say "education of the horse."

"Horses recognize the voices [of their trainers or grooms], even after many years [of separation]." (Kurt Albrecht, former director of the Spanish Riding School).

With a young horse, it is "sending him forward" [*mise en avant*] before "putting him in hand" [*mise en main*].

The training of a young horse consists of passing from relaxation to a certain degree of impulsion, without creating excitement.

144   [Collection is achieved by actions that go from back to front: the roundness of the top line, the engagement and flexion of the hind legs forward UNDER the body and, above all the yielding of the aids (complete lightness of both mouth and haunches) by the mean of the "comprehensive effect." Compression is based on tension achieved by actions that go from front to back (such as the systematically repeated half-halt that brings the body OVER the hind legs and compress their joints)]

145   [A tongue in cheek comment. What Nuno Oliveira also means is that the principles of dressage are few and are simple (such as "Calm, Forward and Straight"), but the details of its execution are many and may take the lifetime of the rider to discover, understand and apply]

146   [which is a word with a connotation of authoritarian training in French]

First objective: relaxation in walk – in trot[147]
Speak [to the horse], caress.
Frequently return to a low neck that stretches down.

First, the young horses must move 1) forward 2) relaxed 3) on long reins. It is only after [all that is routinely achieved] that we can think of [developing] the contact.

Start the young horses by working in natural, forward gaits.

With the young horse, on the circle, we use the inside rein as opening rein (opposite to a trained horse[148]. But little by little, bring him to turn by the action of the seat[149] and advancing the outside shoulder, rather than by the inside rein.

The starting phase of the training of a young horse must pay attention mostly to the mental[150]. We must aim at having a relaxed, calm horse at peace, that doesn't get excited in any of the three gaits. Don't start an exercise until the horse is relaxed. It is only after that [is achieved] that we can start to adjust the reins.

We must pay attention to the mental state of the horse from the start of his relationship with humans, including the delicate approach [of the horse] in the stable.

In the beginning, the young horse must learn to canter on his own, without the help of the aids.

With a young horse, don't ask for a complete shoulder-in, rather for 1/8th of a shoulder-in.

[After a while,] when turning, the young horse must start to bend around the inside leg while keeping his cadence.

With a young horse, first work on the easy side (in the canter for instance), then go to the difficult side and work a little less on that side.

The primary thing for young horses is that in walk, trot and canter, they go
1) well forward[151],
2) without floating[152] and
3) by using themselves [generously].
It is a mistake to "place"[153] the horse with a double bridle; instead,

---

147   [through forward movement]
148   [which we turn by advancing the outside shoulder]
149   [advancing the outside hip]
150   [and emotional aspect of horse's behavior]
151   [in medium gaits on a free rein, with or without a bit]
152   [keeping on straight lines and curves without deviation]
153   [position his front-end and put his forehead on the vertical]

"place" the horse with a snaffle bridle.[154]

In canter, we shouldn't try to cadence a horse that is not [yet] collected.

The first part of training is doing circles and transitions.

Before collecting the horse (by diverse [gymnastic] exercises), we must let the young horse move in ample gaits, quite free, relaxed physically and mentally.

We must hold the whip toward the thigh, [above the stifle] so as not to scare the horse.

With a young horse [actually with all horses], we must try to obtain [training] results without fighting.

In posting trot, the torso must not lean forward, but be more or less vertical.

At the moment of [asking for] transitions, be delicate. Relax your hands. Act as little as possible with the reins. Choose the best moment to ask for the transition, the moment when the horse is calm, relaxed and with good impulsion.

For halts, adjust the reins at such a length that the horse stops by an [upward] action of the torso and not by a traction on the reins. The reins [end up] acting, but by the intermediate action of the torso. This is how we get the young horse used to responding to the action of the torso. Do it first from the walk. Then from a sitting trot that is not too fast.[155] Without blocking the young horse, frame him [in the channel of the aids] so he doesn't float and to can give him the direction you want and not the one he wants.

And this [must be achieved] with movements [from the rider] that don't surprise [the horse].

When you are in posting trot and you feel that the horse is going well, that he doesn't float and that is neck is straight and quiet, sit for a few strides. But in transitioning from the posting trot to the sitting trot, try to slow him down by the fact that you are sitting and not by pulling on the reins. Following that, go back to a bigger trot in posting trot.

To [obtain] the fixity of the poll, we must create accord between the hands and the legs. If the horse lifts his head because the hand is "asleep": take and give, open and close the fingers. But with a young horse, it doesn't matter much if he lifts the poll once by distraction or curiosity. We must feel that the poll is flexible: this [quality] is part of the fixity of

154   [This advice was particularly important in the Iberian Peninsula where riders tend to use the double bridle very early on]
155   [Nuno Oliveira always halted young horses by an upward action that raised the head very slightly and, as a result, lowered the croup a little. As their training progressed, this action was reduced to a simple lifting of the chest]

**Antoine riding Banco, a half-blood Belgian, at Uccle at the
Musette Riding School's Facilities.**

the poll and it's also done partly by the maintenance of a regular cadence.
I agree with the Germans about the fixity of the head, but I don't agree on
their execution[156].

Never let a horse give a kick [in resistance]: [to correct it, use] the
whip, jerk on the reins, [use a] blow of the spur, but collect him first.

The first work with a young horse is to send him forward. It is only
afterwards that we establish cadence.

With a young horse, go in stages. Go from relaxation to a higher
degree of impulsion, but without ever reaching excitement. No strong contact, don't pull on the mouth. To do a circle with a young horse, open the
inside rein. To go from one exercise to the next, don't surprise the horse
(use delicate movements) and prepare [the next exercise] by the quality
of the one that precedes it. Talk [to the horse], caress [often]. Return often
to the low neck [position] and stretch it down.

---

156   [meaning that this fixity should not be achieved early on by a strong
contact, but by the progressive gymnastics of lateral movements]

Draw rein: [we use it] not to lower the head, but to prevent the horse from lifting his poll [if he has that tendency].

After cantering a young horse, go back to posting trot with long reins, push and caress.

The first work with a young horse is physical and mental relaxation, followed by the task of getting him forward. No complicated equitation before the horse moves really forward. The training of a young horse is to go from relaxation to impulsion, without excitement and then back [to relaxation]. There is a limit not to go over. This is how we develop the finesse of the horse [his sensitivity and responsiveness]. Return to relaxation as a reward. Return to walk.

All the young horses must first go 1) forward 2) relaxed 3) on long reins. It is only afterwards that we push the horse on the contact. We must create the mental desire to go forward, so no small gaits with a young horse. We will channel [that energy] later [and start to slow down after the forward desire is well-established].

We cannot work a young horse "in the hand"[157], so we must give [the reins] to help the horse "get longer" [stretch the top line] and then take back delicately.

With a young horse, if we use an "attack of the spur" [to get him more forward], we must release the reins[158]. In canter for example, it is a rule, the horse must go with nothing in his mouth, [no contact]. Loose reins.

With a young horse, proceed progressively, without ever forcing. Otherwise, if his muscular system is not ready [to adopt a more advanced position], we might create resistances. So always think of the "right dose" [of work, of positioning, of impulsion].

We must not ride young horses with short reins.

Young horse: as long as we cannot transition from trot to canter and canter to trot on free reins, in natural gaits, without the help of the aids, we cannot start to "place" the horse [position the front end] or even "train" the horse. We are still in the starting phase. The young horse should not fall back into trot [when being asked to stay in canter] of his own idea, instead he should do it at the moment the rider decides.

Speak to your horse, the voice is an important aid.

With a young horse [while starting the lateral work], we must pay more attention to the push of the haunches than to the bend. First, displace the haunches easily, the bend will come afterwards.

In a group lesson of nervous young horses: "walk while talking

157   [*mise en main*, yet, meaning in position with the forehead on the vertical and light on the bridle]
158   ["Legs without Hands" – Baucher]

and caressing the horses until they return to calmness. It is very important to teach young horses to walk on a loose rein, without abandoning the contact entirely. The first thing is to get them to be relaxed and calm in all three gaits. This is why we must not surprise them by brisk actions nor block them [with the reins too tight]. So, first work in the horizontal balance. It is only as training progresses that we will achieve consistent *mise en main* ["horse in the hand"]. It is only afterwards that we will collect the horse. Otherwise we are building the house on false foundations."

With a young horse, only start the counter-canter when the horse has achieved a certain cadence in the true canter.

With young horses, we help them pass the corners in counter-canter by using [inside] lateral effects [aids]. So in left canter lead tracking right, [use the] right rein and right leg. The horse must be slightly bent right. Send the body of the horse toward the outside left rein[159].

With a young horse, particularly if he is nervous, do not do lessons that are too long.

A young horse cannot and should not have a very short canter. It is only after the horse can stay in a medium canter on his own without running that we can start to control it [and shorten it by collection].

We let the young horse canter naturally, without hand action. We only reduce his canter when [we feel] he can bring his weight onto his hind legs.

With a young horse, it is out of the question to shorten the canter. We must push [forward] instead. We need a natural canter. We only take the reins afterwards, but not before the horse starts to have some self-carriage in the canter.

The young horse needs to first get used to passing from one gait to the other, going forward calmly.

With a young horse, particularly a hot-blooded horse [Thoroughbred , Arabian, Anglo-Arabians, Andalusians, Lusitanos], we must start by making him go in walk, trot and canter on a free rein, without martingale or any [auxiliary rein], except for rare cases. After that, we can start to train the horse [in earnest]. Therefore, we must first establish relaxation.

With a young horse, we cannot start to organize the walk, nor reduce the other gaits before obtaining an energetic and lively forward movement and achieving a strong desire in the horse to go forward.

We must teach all young horses to depart into canter from walk and trot from diverse positions: shoulder-in, counter-shoulder-in, circle around the haunches or voltes around the shoulders.

---

159   [by action of the right leg and by loading the left stirrup slightly forward]

With a young horse [who has learned to go forward freely in the starting phase], we must work first on position and lightness, and the exercises will come later.

With a young horse, it is the hand that gives the direction. When the horse is trained, this role goes to the legs and the hands stay quiet.

Young horse: we will start the trot shoulder-in when the shoulder-in at the walk has become comfortable. And we start the half-pass at the walk when he does his trot shoulder-in really well.

Wanting to reduce the canter of a young horse by the reins is a mistake.

A basic requirement for the young horse is the transition trot – canter – trot, without hands, without legs[160], without compression (on a big circle).

On a young horse at the beginning, we must ask for extended trot in posting trot, until he achieves sufficient suspension and cadence. Otherwise, we will be bouncing in the saddle and it will upset him. Advice for this posting trot: don't set your stirrup leathers too long.

With young horses, we do circles with the inside rein (opening rein). With others [trained horses] it is with the outside rein [advancing the outside shoulder while keeping the outside rein contact].

As training progresses, we diminish the use of the reins for direction and replace it by the legs and the torso.

A good exercise for the canter of a young horse: in a horizontal balance, without any preoccupation of collection and while maintaining the same level of activity, go from trot to canter on a big circle, and return to the trot, not by the reins but by the [action of the] back. Stay only a short time in each gait. It is a better exercise than doing miles in canter.

To obtain the shoulder-in on the long side with a very young horse: walk straight, halt after the second corner of the short side, place him in the shoulder-in position and start again in shoulder-in from the halt.

We can reduce the canter only when the weight is progressively set back on the hind legs[161]. So, with a young horse, stay in free canter.

To help a young horse develop feeling for the influence of the rider's back, we can create the habit for the horse by slightly extending the stride on the long side in posting trot, then allowing the horse to reduce the trot by himself on a circle in sitting trot.

To the very young horse, we only ask for calm halts, not anything else. But pay attention that he starts off again with good straightness.

---

160   [action of the seat and touch of the whip]
161   [by the practice of many lateral gymnastic exercises]

We can only ask for square halts of a horse with [well-developed] impulsion.

For the young horse, the ideal [work session] is:
1) Warm up on the lunge
2) Then supple him in walk
For a older horse, the lunging become less necessary.

With a young horse we only do transitions trot – canter – trot. When these transitions become easy and effortless, we move onto the transition walk – canter – walk (with an energetic, not lifeless canter).

With a young horse, doing the short wall in counter-canter, we use a position close to the shoulder-in. For example: in counter-canter on the left lead and tracking right, we bend the horse to the right on the short side and we pass the corner with lateral aids [right leg, right rein].

With a young horse, only develop the movement ["expressiveness of the gaits"] from a state of relaxation and [a good level] of stability of the head [fixity of the poll]. Trying to develop the movement while [the horse is] in resistance does not get [an increase of] forwardness.[162]

If, with a young horse, we have achieve the transitions "walk – trot – walk" on a circle and then the transitions "trot – canter – trot," he is ready for depart to canter from the walk.

With young horses, we must already pay attention and respect the geometry of the figures, go correctly into corners, and see to it that they don't float too much.

Going trail riding with a young horse that doesn't have the minimum of training is childishness.

The starting of a young horse[163]

The mistakes made during the starting of a young horse are paid during the entire life of the horse. So the starting phase is very important. The rules are simple but imperative.

The starting of the horse must mostly pay attention to the mind of the horse, so try to get him to relax all the time. In order to prepare him to be trained. Pay attention to this [mental] aspect from the beginning and to the rapport between horse and human, including when approaching him in the stable. (Approach him delicately).

In the work, seek the calm and the physical and mental relaxation of the horse.

162   [This is a fundamental piece of advice in times when we see the obsession with the expressiveness of the gaits in young horse classes]
163   ["*debourrage*" translates as "breaking," but we prefer "starting"]

150

It is fundamental to work him in natural gaits, neck lengthened, the horse relaxed, without worrying about placing the head [in any given position].

The young horse must be able to walk, trot and canter in medium gaits, calmly.

He must be able to go through the corners, do circles, halt without getting excited. It is only after all of that [is achieved] in physical and mental relaxation that we can start to adjust the reins and work on collection. It is from that point and not before that we begin the [true dressage] training. It is the base. Those are the foundations on which the building of the training will be constructed. If these foundations are missing, the building will be weak and something will always be missing.

Let's follow the young horse during the normal progression of work:

Lunging: with a three year-old, start the lesson with lunging, using a cavesson and a snaffle[164]. Get the horse used to obeying on the lunge[165] and to respond to the voice for halts, departs, etc.. Pay attention to the quality of the walk: make sure the horse has energy and doesn't sleep. And to the quality of the trot: not a running trot. The horse needs to use himself and that doesn't happen by running or going too fast.

Work on the lunge:

1) Don't start the canter [work] as long as [the horse] resists in the trot against the inside rein [pulls the lunge line by falling outside of the circle], (for instance the right rein when going to the right)[166].

2) In the arena, there are three circles: one at each extremity and one in the center around X[167].

Example of a lunging lesson with a young horse poorly started, not submissive and not dominated by the handler.

The lunge whip must not drag behind the handler but be pointed toward the horse [toward the haunches, not too high].

---

164   [Nuno Oliveira sometimes used side reins when lunging young horses]

165   [increase and decrease the size of the circle]

166   [However the majority of horses fall on the right shoulder, an innate asymmetry that makes them fall to the outside on the left circle (and try to force the contact), as well as make them fall in on the right circle (and not take enough contact on that rein)]

167   [Make sure to move the horse around in the arena while taking some short pieces of straight lines along the long side and practice all three circles in any order, as well as teach the horse to progressively enter in the two corners of the short side]

The whip must not surprise or scare the horse, it should accompany the horse.

Demand of the horse that he enters the corners. Push into canter and maintain the canter until I tell you to return to the trot. Don't go back to trot until the horse is calm and cadenced in canter. The lunge line must be taught [but not with a heavy contact]: we must have a connection with the horse. If the horse cross-canters, release the contact of the lunge a little bit and push [forward] with the lunge whip[168]. Stay in canter until he calms down, becomes balanced and cadences. Stop him by pulling him toward you [so he does a smooth, forward turn toward the handler]. If he moves [in the halt], vibrate the cavesson as strongly as necessary [until he becomes immobile].

Work on the lunge with side reins: (the inside rein must be two holes shorter).

This work should not be done systematically, it all depends on the horse[169]; the duration of the work varies.

[If the horse has not been ridden yet,] we can use this work to get the horse used to the weight of the rider by placing a heavy sack on his back, or even a rider laying across the horse's back like a sack[170].

Sample of the work: start in walk. If the horse moves his head [lack of stability], push delicately [with the lunge whip] to increase the impulsion. If the horse is quiet, try to keep a constant speed, halt him in a corner and wait [for a moment until demonstrates complete immobility and calmness]. We must ask for many halts. Same work [can be done] with the ridden horse [later on].

Return to the walk. In the depart after the halt, use either the lunge whip, or a [little tug on] the lunge line, or take a little step [yourself] in the direction you want the horse to take [use your body language]. Choose the right technique [through trial and error].

The objective to achieve: is that the horse starts into walk from the halt *without lifting his head* (same idea when doing the transition from walk to trot, etc.).

---

168   [When the horse cross-canters, it is advisable to unite the canter again by pushing the horse at the moment he reaches the long side after crossing the middle of the arena, in other words it is when he will feel a little support from the wall on the outside that will entice him to put some weight inside and canter united behind again]

169   [Side reins are a way to start a connection and give the horse some stability in the position]

170   [with a helper supporting the rider by the left leg while the horse is walking]

152

Try to obtain an instantaneous movement forward.

All movements of the head *downward* are good.

Sometimes, by (quietly) lowering the hand that holds the lunge line [and using light vibrations], we can help the head to take the right position.

There needs to be a contact between the hand and the cavesson, so not with a loose lunge line.

Give [release the contact] when the horse releases.

The lunge line is the rein. The lunge whip is the legs. We must have an accord between the two.

Ask for soft transitions between the three gaits, *without movements of the poll* or defenses of the head.

The technique of lunging with side reins must be used without brutality[171].

It is important to achieve the *fixity of the base of the neck* in the transitions. *It is the goal* of the work with side reins.

During the work, see if the horse settles in a constant cadence and position.

When a defense or a resistance occurs, [if for instance the horse quits going forward, faces the handler or pulls away,] and we succeed in sending the horse forward *immediately*, it is a good lesson for the horse [because a latent problem has been solved].

When we are cantering on the lunge, in if the horse gets disunited, what to do? Stop him or push him? That depends on the horse. We can do either, but I give preference to pushing[172].

When lunging, try to obtain square halts[173].

In an arena, there are three circles. In the two circles at the ends, the horse must enter the corners.

All systems (chambon, draw reins, a bit of a shift in the language etc.) should be used momentarily for correcting something and then we return to normal [methods of training] after a few days.

In the following lesson: same work on the lunge line with side reins, now with a rider on his back, (shorten the side reins by one hole). The horse must take contact with the side reins and not the [snaffle] reins

---

171   [The side reins must be adjusted at the right length: not so short that they force the position with a strong contact, not so long that the horse achieves no contact when he is in position]

172   [Release the contact when the horse is facing the wall of the long side and push him with the lunge whip]

173   [By raising the hand slightly in a direction aiming in front of the horse with a small vibration. This is done after the phase in which the horse has learned to halt by facing the handler]

held by the rider. It is best for the rider to hold onto a breast collar or the pommel of the saddle. Same work: halt – walk – trot. Mix the sitting trot with the posting trot (change the diagonal the rider is posting on [frequently]). When the horse becomes calm and rounded [in his top line], the rider must caress often.

We must not allow the horse to diminish the circle on his own, but only when the handler holding the lunge line wants it [otherwise the horse is falling on his inside shoulder and losing impulsion].

When the horse is comfortable with the lunging work, it will be useful to make him jump a little cavaletti or a little fence (without side reins or rider), or even without a lunge line, at liberty, if the arena is enclosed[174].

Any auxiliary rein (Chambon, draw reins or bit with tongue liberty) must be used temporarily to correct a problem and then we return to normal [equipment] after a few days.

"Work-in-hand" of the young horse (from the ground): if it is well done, it can really advance the training work and help us reach a whole new level of domination. But this work can only be practiced by experienced riders who possess a lot of tact.

[Nuno Oliveira:] "In the book *Reflections on Equestrian Art*, I say "the work in hand is very complex and I advise the riders who do not have a great practice of dressage and who are not familiar with it to leave it well alone."

This work collects the horse further.

The tone of the voice is very important.

The whip pushes [by touches] and calms down [by pressure]. It is important in the work-in-hand to halt the horse by [pressure of] the whip on the loins.

What I think we must look for is a horse that walks with the minimum of aids and stays round. If he puts weight [on the hand], do some small vibrations [on the reins]. He must halt without being open [disengaged], round, straight, without resistance.

He must move without making any force [against the hand of the handler] in the slowest walk possible.

Nature of the walk: walk straight – halts – shoulder-in – little circles in shoulder-in, etc.

Comment: this work can be followed by ridden work with the goal that the horse associates the brush of the whip with the action of the rider's leg that is approaching softly.

---

174   [This jumping work increases both the balance and the impulsion of the horse]

First lesson of the horse ridden at liberty [off the lunge line].

The first lesson's goal is to teach him the response to the reins. This lesson is in walk and posting trot.

To keep him along the wall, keep the outside rein a little opened and taught [connection] like an opening rein, and at the same time hold the whip against the inside shoulder to push the front-end against the wall.

To turn: switch rein, so open the inside rein while keeping the whip on that side. All of that is done delicately.

The first time [that the horse is turned loose], it is useful to place two aides in the arena at G and D[175].

During the trot work, ask for a few moments of faster trot and the next day, ask for a few minutes of canter.

The first leg aid we must teach the horse: on the circle, with the inside leg at the girth, roll the calf from back to front in the direction of the movement[176].

The following lessons will consist of increasing the degree of submission of the horse by "going large" around the arena on the track, doing some well designed circles, changes of direction on the diagonal, figure eights and paying attention that all the figures be well-designed and that the horse enters all the corners, passing everywhere the rider wants him to go.

The trot will be done posting with good energy, but not running. Sometimes do some sitting trot on the circles.

From the posting trot, push the horse until he falls softly into an ample canter on a circle before going around the arena [going large]. Finish the lesson by walking on a loose rein and doing some halts[177].

When the young horse is disciplined in all these exercises and will do his figures with good geometry and without revolt, we will be able to ask him some steps of quarters-out on the circle [leg yield] by using inside lateral aids (on the right rein, use the right leg and the right rein acting toward the left). As soon as he gives, go forward on the circle [on one track] as a reward.

Little by little, progressively we will achieve some slight shoulder-

---

175 [at both ends of the arena. The aides must carry a lunge whip each and figure out how much impulsion they must create by their discrete actions to complement the impulsion created by the actions of the rider using the riding whip]

176 [The impulsion created by the leg must be supported (or replaced in case the horse doesn't respond acceptably) by the rider using the riding whip if necessary]

177 [by raising the hands gently, just as was done on the lunge line]

ins on the long side (this position is called *"placé fléchie droit"* or "placed with [round] flexion-straight" [and is often referenced by the riders of the Spanish Riding School who practice it a lot]) and later, we will arrive at the true lateral work.

The lesson of *"the nose on the ground"*[178].

With the snaffle, it can be done with or without draw reins.

This work is particularly indicated for horses with a high set neck and a hollow back, but it is good for all young horses.

Let's suppose we are doing the work with a snaffle and the draw reins. It is important to note that in this case, the draw reins are used to lower the head and obtain the *ramener* [verticality of the forehead]. This is contrary to its normal use [which is only to prevent the horse from lifting his head too high].

The principle consists of pushing the horse with the legs (first in trot) and play with the draw reins until the horse lowers his head and lifts his back.

Immediately reward and cease the action of the draw reins.

Various gaits can be used: medium trot sitting, working trot posting, walk, canter.

Also various figures: go large [around the arena], circles, figure eights, serpentines (more or less tight).

In walk, do tight circles while playing with the draw reins, particularly the inside one while giving on the outside one, so the horse looks at the center of the circle while lowering his head. We must feel that he lifts and "gives" his back. On the circle, play with the inside rein as an opening rein.

Note: we will do the opposite with the trained horses. With them, we will use the inside rein as little as possible.

In trot: before we start playing with the [inside] rein, we need to push the horse forward with the legs; the horse must be really forward. If we do not push forward before the action of the rein, it will detract from the impulsion.

Push also if the horse wants to do the hovering trot or the passage-like trot.

[The work of] the nose on the ground must be done in an energetic trot and not a trot that lacks impulsion.

Golden rule: for the young horses in this work

1) create forwardness and

---

178   [This is for a horse well confirmed in the connection, the discipline of the figures and a beginning of lateral work]

2) work the nose on the ground.

The *ramener* will come by itself. It is an equitation from "back to front."

Don't go from the sitting trot to the posting trot if the horse has the head up in the air. Only do that if he has lowered his nose.

In the volte [small circle], the weight of the rider must not fall to the outside.

To push the horse forward, use the legs, but do so with aids of decreasing strength because if we act all the time [with the same intensity], we will render the horse dull and put him to sleep.

If the horse is lazy, push more. If he is lively, try to obtain the slowest possible cadence.

[For the exercise of the nose on the ground], don't forget the [absolute] necessity of pushing the horse forward, otherwise the exercise is ineffective. It is by the impulsion of the hind legs that we obtain the lowering of his head. Use this technique [pushing forward with the leg] until the horse can do an entire long side with his nose on the ground by himself without the rider having to use the reins.

Justification of this technique [of the nose on the ground]: the back is the link between the forehand and the hind-end. In nature, the horse is naturally supple [enough to do everything he needs to do]. When we put the weight of the rider on his back, we change his entire equilibrium, particularly if the rider pulls on the reins. From this [problem] comes our concept of how to work the young horse and of the importance of the back that needs to lift [the rider]. [Working with the nose on the ground is the best way to obtain this result]. The rider must not have the sensation that he is sitting in a hollow [that doesn't support him effectively].

After a while, we can alternate the draw reins and the snaffle rein until the horse maintains the same position [nose down] and the same cadence [due to his newly acquired balance] only with the snaffle rein.

[During this work] only halt with the nose on the ground[179]. If during that work we need to "contain" the horse [if he loses his balance], don't do it by pulling on the reins but by using the torso [upwards] in the classical manner and bringing the waist forward toward the hands [adjustment of the balance of the horse by modification of the rider's position], then release after the horse slows down [return to the normal position of the torso and soften the hands]. Eventually, you may use "concrete hands"[180]

179   [by an action of the torso coming up and the seat becoming heavy and a release of the contact]
180   [hands that resist completely in opposition to the loss of balance but without pulling back]

nendations: depart into trot from the position of the nose in walk. [Alternately], we can also depart into trot from a shoulder-in on a walk circle.

In small circles in walk, it is important that the horse doesn't throw any excess weight neither to the inside nor to the outside and doesn't place his head in a crooked position. We must indicate the direction of the volte by the inside leg. It is important that the horse doesn't resist the inside leg by leaning on it [become glued to it]. He must turn bent and soft in all the parts of his body, including his neck and his jowl, and all the parts of his body must be correctly lined up [no crookedness].

At no time [in this work] shall we abandon the contact, the intensity of the contact must stay the same [very light but present]. When we want to lower the neck on the circle, we must not abandon but keep the same intensity of contact. It is a displacement of contact [by a movement of our hand forward and downward], not an abandonment. It is the impulsion that makes the horse lower his neck while staying on the circle.

(We would be well-advised to make marks on the draw reins, so their length is the same on both sides).

The walk and the trot must be slow and relaxed, energetic but without running.

At the end of the lesson: walk on a loose rein and stop when the horse stretches his neck [completely].

During the work, as we are busy working the back of the young horse, don't allow him to lift his poll and put his head up in the air. If he lifts his head, close your fingers, fix the hand and push forward onto [the contact of] the draw reins, and give when he releases, [be sure] to work until he gives himself [relaxes his back and lifts it without tension].

Don't let him come out of the head position [that you want, which is stretched down].

Don't let the reins float. If needed[181], tap with the whip.

Go from trot to canter on the circle, without the horse moving his head.

If the horse sometimes lacks energy in the work, use the *method that is sometimes called the "De Salins Method"* (see his book: *Epaule en dedans, Secret de l'Art de l'équestre* "Shoulder-in, Secret of Equestrian Art, by Comandant J. de Salins"). It is, simply put, a method of putting the horse forward.

Comment: this method can be used without draw reins.

This work consists in doing transitions trot – canter – trot – canter,

---

181   [more impulsion or more relaxation]

with the horse truly forward, in such a way that the horse gives h... well-rounded.

Technique: the horse on a circle in canter to the right, to get int... trot, push the haunches to the outside by opening the right rein to the right and downward, and by pushing with the right leg [leg yield to the left]. The right leg can be placed a little further back. We also need to release the left rein. We are using the right (inside) lateral aids.

It is not so much the delicacy of the aid that matters but rather its energy and intensity: the haunches must be pushed forward and to the left and the horse must fall on the right shoulder-into trot without holding back. He must transition instantly, without hesitation, into a strong, *energetic* trot. Then go back from trot into canter on the circle.

Go back to trot again in the same way. When he gives a trot with impulsion, cease the aids and give the reins so the horse can stretch his nose to the ground.

"When trained to go forward that way, the horse has no longer any desire to resist."

It is obtaining forwardness before seeking to put the horse in the hand [ramener]. *C'est la "mise en avant" avant la "mise en main."*

Chambon.[182]

Example of a lunge lesson:

Lunge the young horse without attaching the Chambon. After a few rounds on the lunge, attach the Chambon [quite loose to begin with]. The lunge must be attached to the cavesson[183]. First work in walk, then get the horse into [a slow] trot.

Work calmly in a little (*petit*) trot so the horse releases his back.

Then do many transitions from walk to trot and trot to walk. The nose must be as low to the ground as possible[184]. The ideal to obtain is that the horse does the transitions [walk – trot – walk] with the nose on the ground.

After that work, take the Chambon off and ride the horse with a draw rein.

---

182   [An auxiliary rein to be used in the case of a horse that really needs to work downward because of a high neck set and hollow back].

183   [Make sure there is enough space between the corners of the lips and the cavesson's nose band, so the horse doesn't get pinched when the bit rides up under the early effect of the Chambon].

184   [Quiet impulsion produced by little actions of the whip is the main factor in making the horse lower his head. Above all, do not surprise the horse with the whip so he doesn't throw his head up]

en to riders working with young horses:

is to do a work that develops the flexibility of the horse
hat compresses him.

nything else, we work on the physical relaxation and the
s that will give the young horse the state of mind necessary to accept the dressage training later on.

With a young horse, perfect the trot by making many changes of direction (serpentines, etc.) and use weight aids principally. This approach develops mobility in the horse.

Do a natural canter with ample strides, without rushing.

At the beginning of the lesson, walk until you feel that the horse is deeply relaxed, gives his back and is truly forward. In short, march in a good, relaxed walk.

When the young horse goes from trot to canter and canter to trot, we must not let him mark a halting moment.

At the beginning of the lesson [group lesson with several young horses working together], the teacher asks for the young horses to be ridden in a warm-up trot (posting) and insists on obtaining as long a neck as possible. However, even in this trot, try to maintain the cadence and pay attention to the flexibility [of the back] in trot serpentines. (In the posting trot, don't lean forward. Keep the torso more or less vertical).

To another rider, he says: "it is too early to work this young horse all the time in the hand [*mise en main*]. It is alright [to do it] from time to time when you feel that the poll is flexible. Otherwise, let the neck stretch out."

To the same rider: "be delicate in the transitions trot – canter – trot. At the moment of the transitions, use the reins as little as possible. Relax the hands. And in order to have delicate aids and to not have to push too much when going from trot to canter, choose the moment when the trot is full of impulsion and the horse is calm and relaxed. Don't canter with the horse in position [forehead on the vertical] before achieving really easy transitions and a relaxed canter."

Again to same rider on a circle to the right: "your transitions trot – canter are not soft enough. Hold the snaffle reins more than the curb (he advises him to ride the horse the next time on a simple snaffle). Your mare tosses her head [resists by lifting her head brutally] because you are trying to get her too collected [too soon]. Open the right snaffle rein to the right and push the horse with the inside (right) leg so the horse gets into canter with the nose lower. She must take the canter with a neck that is long and lowered. Go back to trot when the horse offers a soft contact and not when her head is moving [out of control]."

160

More advice: "in the warm up posting trot, caress the neck, left side, then on the right side, but without letting go of the rein. It is of the ways to get an extension of the neck.

Criticism of another rider: "in your transitions canter - trot, you abandon [the contact] too much. You must push when you do a down transition. When he starts the trot, the horse must come "up to the hand."

Advice to riders training young colts at the very beginning of their training.

To one rider: "you are going too fast. In this cadence, the horse moves his head. Try to find the cadence in which the horse has a better [and more stable] position.

To another: "with your horse, without blocking him, adjust one rein, then the other, more to the right, then more to the left, keep changing, alternate the reins so your horse floats less. By this technique, get the horse to go in the direction you want, not the direction he chooses. In short, frame him [between the reins] to give him a better [more stable] direction."

To another: "try to have more cadence in the walk. It is a bit too fast. Start a circle and then change directions [repeatedly] until the walk cadence improves. Try to get a slower, shorter walk."

To the same rider attempting a shoulder-in (1/8 of shoulder-in [at this stage of training]): "the horse is resisting, so don't insist. Do a very small walk circle [first] and then return to the shoulder-in. Sometimes halt in the position of the shoulder-in before starting it again."

To another working at the trot: "the cadence is too fast, [the horse] moves his head too much. Try to see in which cadence he gets the best positions of the head, that will be the right cadence. At this stage, the [right] trot is the one in which the horse is the most comfortable, even if the horse is a little "flat." Later, when we will be looking for impulsion and collection, the criteria for the quality of the trot will be a little different. For now, we must be looking for the tempo in which the horse is the most at ease."

To another also working in trot: "do some serpentines [in posting trot] in the slowest and shortest trot possible, with a relaxed horse. If you see him relaxed and quiet, find out if he allows you to demand a little more contact, if you can have the reins a little more taught, and then do a few strides of sitting trot. With a young horse, we should work 85% in posting trot and 15% in sitting trot. When we feel that the horse is going really well, that he is not floating and his neck is well-positioned and stable, then we sit so we can feel his back in sitting trot for a few strides."

When passing from posting trot to sitting tot, try to slow [the

…on the
…one

…ıe fact you are sitting and not by pulling on the reins.

…me of sitting trot], increase the trot again by going back

…: "avoid having your hands too static. Try to find the best
…them, within a small space, so the horse is the lightest.

…ır: "don't insist to halt your horse at the exact place where
he doesn't want to halt and is fighting you, but, for example, do a couple of circles or a serpentine and then ask him again to halt."

To another: "because the left side is less easy (the one that is the heaviest and you find the most difficult to bend), he is most likely to resist the left rein and let go of the contact on the right rein. *Rule:* don't resist on the left rein and fight him. That would result in an endless fight. Instead, hold the left rein lightly and play on the rein with your fingers and try to keep the contact on the right side. It is a rule that works with all the horses.

At the beginning [of training] of the young horse, there are two things we shouldn't lose sight of: 1) impulsion and 2) relaxation.

With a horse that is not yet trained, ask for the canter depart without collecting the horse.

When cantering a young horse on a free rein, we must insist that the horse places his nose to the inside in the corners and not bend outward.

With a horse that is not yet very advanced [in training], do a calm canter, with very little hand aids and pass from one gait to the next (canter – trot – canter) without the horse losing his impulsion.

Alternate trot and canter in forward movement.

Before anything else [before putting the horse on the contact and starting gymnastic movements], we need a horse that is in impulsion, straight, light, relaxed [in all three gaits].

Seek to achieve perfection in simple exercises right from the beginning of the training.

With a beginner horse, canter without collecting the horse too much, but also not too much on the forehand.

As long as a horse cannot do a figure eight in a free canter while staying on the same lead, we cannot start any other exercise in canter [such as anything to do with the collection of the canter: half-passes, shoulder-ins, halts from canter, etc.].

If we start the complicated things too soon before the horse knows how to walk, trot and canter quietly (but naturally with impulsion), we will start a fight that never ends.

With a young horse, we do not yet speak of "the horse in hand," but we must obtain a position of the head that is nearly immobile and corresponds to a constant position of the front-end.

With a young horse, don't start the counter-canter before obtaining [work] in true canter that is balanced and canter departs [from the trot] that are calm. Otherwise you may well get the counter-canter, but it will be by force.

First order with a young horse: work in a forward, natural movement.

One of the first principles to teach [the young horse] is to never resist the [request] for forward movement.

We must not "corner" a young horse [between the aids], he must remain mentally relaxed. And to see if he is really in that state, observe his eye, his ears, etc. [examine his attitude].

A general rule is that, on a circle, it is important to use the inside rein as little as possible. However that is mostly true for trained horses. For the young horses, we need to use the inside rein as an opening rein. (Same thing for the work with the draw reins with a young horse).

In the training process of a young horse, we must not ask for the *ramener* [forehead on the vertical] before obtaining that the horse be completely relaxed.

With a young horse, do frequent halts, and before starting again calmly, wait for him to spend a few moments of immobility, "in peace." Also do many transitions, particularly walk to trot, trot to walk, as well as trot – canter, canter – trot.

With a young horse, get him used to reducing the speed a little by passing from posting trot to sitting trot, but achieve it by the fact that the rider sits down, not by pulling on the reins.

The "starting phase" of a young horse must focus particularly on the mental state of the horse. It is "preparing" him to be trained. We must aim at having a relaxed horse.

With a young horse, it is not a good idea to ask for a full shoulder-in but, by displacing the seat [laterally] (rather than by using reins and legs), ask for 1/8 of a shoulder-in at the beginning.

Make a particular effort to have the young horse in the same state of mind in the three gaits (walk – trot – canter), calm, at peace and not excited.

If the young horse has a more difficult side [which is to be expected], for example in canter, work first on the easy side, then go to the difficult side and work that side for less time than the easy side.

The last impressions of the horse [the last thing he does in the lesson] (before returning to his stall and meditate) are very important [because that is what he will remember]. Try to obtain that he calmly puts his nose on the ground just after the last halt.

The end of the lesson in draw reins for a young horse consists of walking on a long rein and stop when the horse stretches his neck down.

With a young horse, use the lateral aids that help the horse lengthen his frame (instead of the diagonal aids that engage the horse and help him sit [for collection]).

With a young horse, practice a walk that is not yet collected, and mostly pay attention:

1) To the regularity of the cadence

2) That he stays cadenced not only in straight lines but also that in turns, the horse bends properly around the inside leg while keeping his cadence.

With a young horse, only start an exercise if he is relaxed and not rushing. If needed, do a few voltes to calm him before starting the exercise.

Antoine, riding Faudo: start of the Passage.

With a young horse do turns more by using the seat and by advancing the outside shoulder than by using the inside rein.

With a young horse, an excellent exercise is to do a counter-shoulder-in along the wall, and after the second corner, change rein on the diagonal in shoulder-in. At the end of the diagonal, let the horse lower his neck progressively at each step.

With a young horse, small gait variations are more likely to keep his interest up and keep him active than kicking him with spurs.

The training of a young horse starts by using a position that is natural and relaxed.

The first thing for young horses is that in walk – trot – canter, they go really forward by using themselves, without floating.

With a young horse, in a trot circle for instance, feel that he is really giving on the inside [bends and engages].

With a young horse in a canter circle, go back to trot by mostly us-

Start of the Piaffe.

ing the inside leg and inside rein[185].

To obtain the bend in the corner, use the inside leg near the girth sliding from back to front and not the inside rein.

From time to time, with a young horse, to finish the lesson, get into sitting trot, fix the hand by closing the fingers (but don't bring the hand backward [ABSOLUTELY DO NOT PULL]) and push the horse on the hand. Wait for the horse to give in his neck and come up on the hand [arches his neck and lifts it slightly into a better position].

With a young horse, after work in impulsion (in walk, trot and canter), proceed in a natural gait with the neck extended. This when the horse is relaxed. It is from that point on that we can start the dressage training and not before.

It is a mistake to position a young horse by using the full bridle. We must place the young horse with the snaffle (by doing varied exercises: voltes, shoulder-in, lengthening and shortening of the gaits, etc.) When he is positioned ["placed"] in the snaffle, then we can put the full bridle on.

In canter, we must no try to cadence a horse[186] that is not yet collected. This would create the risk of taking away his impulsion. He will learn to become cadenced progressively.

With horses that are not yet advanced, do the work of the transitions canter – trot with relatively free reins, with half-taught reins.

The young horse must walk –trot – canter in medium gaits. It is only afterwards that we start to adjust the reins and work on collection, after we have obtained the physical and mental relaxation of the horse.

For the work of young horses, the principle is "hands without legs, legs without hands." It is the opposite of the "comprehensive effect" ["*effet d'ensemble*"] used with more advanced horses to obtain collection. "Hands without legs" is used to teach him to "know" his mouth, to obey the reins, but without going as far as the "comprehensive effects."

"Legs without hands" consists of pushing the young horse without slowing him down, so as not to reduce his gait, and to send him forward [developing the forward desire of the horse].

"Without hands" doesn't mean that we should abandon the reins, because even with a young horse, the reins must be adjusted, but only with a light contact.

Before collecting the horse (by different exercises), we must leave the young horse in medium gaits, quite free, mentally and physically relaxed. If we position the horse [on the vertical] too soon, the back will not function and we will end up with a horse "in two pieces."

185   [One of the ways to get a canter-trot transition is to release the inside rein, push with the inside leg and let the horse fall on that shoulder]
186   [slow him down]

166

We can keep a young horse collected in the trot, but it takes much longer [to achieve it] in the canter.

Consider the length of the stirrup leathers on a young horse.

-In trot, we are shaken more and we must do posting trot, so shorten the leathers by two holes.

-In canter, with a young horse that is not yet collected, we must not ride with stirrups that are too long, otherwise we are always out of balance.

It is by perfecting the quality of the transitions, by respecting all the small details of the transitions, that we prepare the collection with young horses. [If we don't do it that way] we will have to use some [artificial] techniques. From this stems the need for soft and correct transitions.

Note from the book *Reflections on Equestrian Art*: "what is necessary in transitions is to fix the base of the neck."

With a young horse, we must try to obtain results without a fight.

Example of a lesson: trot a young horse under saddle.

On the circle: from the shoulder-in in walk, pass to trot shoulder-in for a few strides, then return to the normal trot [on single track].

While going large [around the arena]: trot – halt – trot. Prepare the halt [carefully].

Variations in the trot (for a few strides). Reduce the gait by the action of the torso, without losing the vibration of the trot, and without suddenness.

From the shoulder-in at the trot on the circle, proceed to the volte around the haunches and then to the half-pass on the diagonal (horse in lightness, without changing the cadence).

Rules:

-Inside rein light,

-Same dose of energy,

-Only do the transitions when the horse is light and when we master the cadence.

Example of a lesson: canter of a young horse.

Don't insist [on long sessions], do only short periods of canters.

Example: depart with the head turned in the direction of the lead. Change to the opposite bend and return to the true bend[187].

Depart [into canter] after a very small circle in shoulder-in, and before he gets open, finish the circle with haunches-in[188].

187   [keep changing the bend every few strides by advancing the hand on the outside of the bend]

188   [support each bend with a little pressure of the inside leg]

While going large: Depart into true canter after a reinback;
In this canter:
a) Nose to the left, nose to the right,
b) Attempt at a slight shoulder-in.
Depart in counter-canter and also do nose to the right, nose to the left.

In the circle in canter: attempt a slight shoulder-in, then volte around the haunches; [same bend]. Change the bend and repeat in the other direction.

Canter head to the wall [travers/haunches-in] with correct bend. Half-pass in canter [on a diagonal], with correct bend.

Passade[189]

Try to change leg from true canter to counter-canter at the beginning of the long side[190].

Change from counter-canter to true canter on the circle[191].
Variations of the gait in canter.
a) Extend on the long side and come back on the circle.
b) Go to a figure eight while alternating the two bends.

To improve the canter of a young horse:
Transitions on the circle trot – canter – trot (done with the seat).
-Canter circles while changing the bend.
-Vary [the size] of the circles.
-The canter half-pass is used to collect the canter.

Example of a lesson to a young horse the Master sees for the first time. This horse in October 1987 is three and a half, he already knows the saddle, has been ridden and is well-started.

The rider/owner is not a beginner and therefore does not receive basic advice regarding the position, etc.. The lessons are given as a func-

---

189   Note: from Baucher's "Equestrian pastimes": "Passade: we can, without neglecting the true principles of equitation, get one's horse to execute a few passades. They have no inconveniences for the art and offer a real utility for the military horse."

Baucher: "Reasoned Dictionary of Equitation": "The passade is the name of various movements voltes, detours and returns that the horse can execute in canter, by passing rapidly from one point to the other."

[The classical passade in the 18th century was a series of two opposite half-turns with a flying change in between.]

190   [creates less flexion of the new inside leg, therefore it is easier]

191   [creates more flexion of the new inside leg, therefore it is harder]

tion of the young horse's needs and are about his behavior. After having observed him the first day ridden by his owner, Master Oliveira directs the lessons the following days.

First lessons (October 87)

1) The horse on the lunge, first without side-reins, and then with the side-reins "to adjust him and support him better" [begin to create a position].

Advice about lunging:

-Elastic tension of the lunge.

-Don't let the horse come to the inside of the circle.

-Maintain a regular gait.

-Rustling of the wrist [vibration] if the horse moves his head or doesn't yield.

-Watch the feet of the horse: see if they show energy and good cadence.

-When the horse is cantering, if he goes back to trot by himself, get back to canter immediately.

2) Work-in-hand, trying to make the horse "come up" on the hand (role of the outside rein). Push onto the hand just until he rounds.

3) Follow by mounted work. Ask a helper to hold the lunge attached to the cavesson. Attempt at shoulder-in by association of the whip (held by the helper on the ground) and the leg (used by the rider). It is the rider who initiates the demand; the helper walks slightly in front of the horse, and not crowding the horse. March in shoulder-in on a circle, then on the long side and finally on a diagonal (still in shoulder-in). The helper walks backwards in front of the horse and not alongside him.

Example: a 4 year old horse, equipped with a snaffle.

First on the lunge: when he starts to play, get crooked and lean to the inside of the circle, we need to push him on the hand. Ask for more trot than canter.

Ridden work: Nuno Oliveira says "He is floating and playing a little, at this stage, that's normal. He is passing from the kindergarten to elementary school. It is the moment to demand a little more from our pupil, to adjust him and expect more from his position and his impulsion.

Auxiliary rein: we will use the snaffle and the draw reins. The draw reins are not used to pull, but to fix the horse and adjust him, to prevent him from putting his head everywhere, to prevent him from lifting his head in the transitions, to fix [the base of] his neck. Carry two whips to avoid having to pass the whip from one side to the other.

Put him in an energetic posting trot without letting him canter.

Adjust the draw reins. Push with both whips toward the back, hold the hand fixed until the poll rounds up. Don't release until he releases his poll.

Push [forward] more with the whips than with the legs. Don't let him canter but maintain the energetic trot (not a short trot). Today's [job], consists of adjusting [the horse], sending him forward without letting his head move around. In the left circle, open the left rein a little bit to the left. Don't let the poll come up. Play a little bit with the draw reins if needed to help the poll get rounder. Don't reduce the trot, I don't want any canter today. What I want is that the poll stays placed with an energetic trot. I don't want the horse to rush, but I don't want him lose energy either. If needed, play with the draw reins while pushing [the horse forward]. No canter, no shoulder-in. Today, it's putting the horse forward in discipline, while avoiding him holding back. Go large and in big circles. Push until the poll releases and becomes stable, and that the horse no longer wants to change his position.

In the circle, we use the draw reins on the outside and we push with the whip on the inside haunch. When he releases, the rider also releases immediately. The problem is that the majority of riders do not release in time. We must cease our action when the horse releases and see [that we use] the right dose [of action and release needed]. Release for as long as possible without abandoning the horse. If we release too little, the horse will resist. If we release too much, the horse falls on the forehand. Objective: maintain the lightness. (Note: this work is a commentary on the rule: "push, hold and give").

Do a large figure eight, then take the diagonal.

Tomorrow, you will use a pair of light spurs. Then you will push also with the spurs [in association with the action of the whips].

The next day: the horse is first worked on the lunge, then ridden with the draw reins. Start with a big trot. Then push into canter on a circle. Go back to the energetic trot. The horse must not canter of his own accord. (If he does that by himself, it would demonstrate a lack of impulsion).

Canter again in a circle, go large in canter and do another circle at the other end. Take the diagonal in canter inside lead, and do the short side in counter-canter (in his big canter). Trot again. "Push more with a light, sharp tap of the whip."

Transition to an energetic walk. Shoulder-in on the long side. Back to trot immediately. Change rein and energetic walk again in shoulder-in on the other long side. "He must do all of that work without holding back." Trot again and change rein. Walk (push, hold and give; remember: push before holding). Caress the horse and take the center line. Continue to do transitions trot – canter – walk – shoulder-in. It is pointless to do miles of trot "bang – bang – bang." Fix the hand and don't let the horse do the transition into trot with his head up in the air.

In walk, take the center line walk a few steps in a straight line and then walk sideways toward the wall. Repeat this exercise several times.

Trot: adjust [the reins] a little more and try to reduce the trot a little bit, without diminishing the energy. Do a serpentine in posting trot, then sitting trot and halt.

"We will soon take the draw reins off as they will no longer be necessary."

Next day's work: same as the day before, start with lunging, then ridden (again with the draw reins). Working trot rising (the working trot is an energetic trot). Reduce the trot a little but keep the same energy[192]. Sit the trot and do a few lateral steps, not half-passes. A lateral step is neither a half-pass nor a shoulder-in [more like a leg yield]. Pay attention to the reins and keep the horse straight while marching slightly sideways, advancing forward and staying as much as possible, parallel to the wall. The head stays straight and avoid crookedness. Press the whip very lightly on the [outside] haunch, to activate the haunches [laterally].

(Note: If the horse leans on the rein on the side of the bend during a half-pass and places his head in a crooked position, we must return to the lateral steps [straight body, no bend] and only return progressively to the half-pass later.)

Go back to posting trot and then canter on the circle. Go large in canter. Take the diagonal with a minimum of rein aid and counter-canter on the short side (use the leg on the inside of the arena) [and keep the weight on the stirrup outside the arena to keep that shoulder loaded]. Trot again and alternate posting trot and sitting trot.

Go back to walk and do a shoulder-in on the long side followed the center line at A and a few lateral steps (still in walk) [and returning to the wall]. [When reaching the wall] counter-shoulder-in in walk [head to the wall], straighten the horse and walk on a loose rein. Halt [on a loose rein, just load the seat]. During the halt, place the horse [position the head on the vertical] and depart into walk without any movement of the head. Do the same thing on the center line at X [halt and depart with head fixed], the horse really straight. Repeat [these halts and departs] until obtaining complete straightness.

Advice: at the end of the lesson, it might be useful sometimes to do some cavaletti, first on the lunge line, then ridden in a little relaxed trot

---

192   [and do not go do to a collected trot]

(so he can release his back) and without side reins, so he can lengthen his neck.

Other advice: given occasionally to the riders:

- Lightness doesn't exist without impulsion.

- Don't allow the neck to get crooked at the base: [use] the reins to compensate [that tendency].

- Supporting the canter with the outside rein is the way to straighten the neck and to keep it straight.

Canter with a beginning horse.

With a young horse, use the medium canter, and if you want to slow it down, do so only moderately. The young horse in canter must not "repeat"[193] and throw his legs upwards [a potential problem with Iberian horses]. We must only slow down when the rider feels the horse staying round [in his top line]. At the beginning, the horse must learn to canter on his own without the support of the aids.

Sample exercise: balance the horse [from back to front] by enlarging and shortening the trot alternately through the action of the waist, while keeping the same tempo, the same cadence, i.e. the same tac-tac of the metronome, without any action of the arms and without any change in the position [of the front-end].

Same work in canter, but prudently: don't slow down too much and don't enlarge [the stride] too much either, [to avoid] putting the horse too much on the forehand.

Rules for the study of counter-canter with a young horse

With a young horse, don't start the counter-canter before obtaining balance in the true canter and calm departs [from the trot]. Otherwise, the counter-canter will be forced. For the counter-canter, we need a small degree of collection.

For the usefulness of the counter-canter, see *Reflections on Equestrian Art* by Nuno Oliveira.

For clarity, *let's talk about a canter on the right lead, tracking left,* (this will avoid the confusion about terms such as "inside" and "outside"). With a young horse [capable of a leg yield], we will maintain the left bend, toward the inside of the arena [bending with the direction of going, not with the lead]. We will progressively invert the bend in proportion with the degree of collection achieved, to eventually arrive at the normal right bend [bending with the lead] with the trained horse [capable of a canter

---

193   [canter up and down like a sewing machine]

half-pass].

1) It is important to maintain the same tempo of canter to prevent the horse from rushing his canter to stay in counter-canter.

2) When changing rein on the diagonal, we must reach the wall well before the corner. We must avoid surprising the horse by the [sharpness of the] corner. So when starting the diagonal, aim at the exact place you want to reach [the less experienced the horse, the further away from the corner you should aim] and bend the horse around the left leg.

3) The entire body of the horse must reach the wall, not just the shoulders. Hence the importance of supporting the horse with the left leg[194].

4) We must keep the horse very close to the wall and make him enter the corner as in a shoulder-in. If the horse goes away from the wall on the short side, the horse will fall on the left shoulder.

5) We must therefore send the horse from left to right and load the right shoulder on which the horse canters. So stop using all the actions of the lateral aids on the right. Abandon the right rein and free the right shoulder [so it can extend forward and slightly to the right]. Abandon also all action of the right leg (eventually take the spur away for a rider who doesn't have enough control of the independence of his leg aids).

Once the right side is freed up, [really moving forward to cover the extra ground on the outside of the turn], we must now close the left shoulder and control it so the horse doesn't fall to the inside. This is done by using the left lateral aids and by keeping the bend to the left toward the inside of the arena.

We can place the nose slightly to the left as soon as we meet the wall after the change of hand on the diagonal. We shouldn't leave the horse abandoned [no contact] nor let him float [lose the consistency of the direction].

6) Obviously, place the whip in the left hand.

7) Be one with the horse and use the torso to help the horse [in the movement of the canter and the direction of the exercise]. Accompany the movement by advancing the [rider's] right shoulder and turning the head toward the inside of the arena.

8) We can progressively *prepare* [the counter-canter] by the following exercise: start in a short trot on the right rein and take the diagonal in left shoulder-in reaching the middle of the long side (at B)[195]. Do it sev-

194   [and pushing the haunches very slightly to the right/outside. Also very important is to keep the weight on the right stirrup to keep the right shoulder slightly loaded so the horse remains vertical and to prevent him from changing lead in front.]

195   [You can push the exercise one step further and do a left circle that is

eral times until the horse offers no resistance.

Then do the same in canter. After cadencing the horse on the circle [to the right] take the diagonal with the horse bent left.

Next step: after [the counter-canter] change rein again and go back to trot when reaching the long side.

9) The next time, go back to trot a little further away (and caress), and every time after that, [canter] a little further.

We can also help prepare the counter-canter by doing the long side before changing rein [to go into counter-canter in right canter on the right direction in a left] counter-shoulder-in in canter to bring the right shoulder out. Advise the rider to let go of the reins a little bit in case the horse leans a little.

The geometry of the figures helps discipline the horse. Otherwise the horse gains some bad habits, such as falling on one shoulder or another, etc.

The rider has finally understood what a half-pass really is when he understands that the inside leg is more important than the outside leg. Because if [the rider can start the half-pass with the position of the torso and the help of the outside rein and] there is no need for the outside leg, it is because the horse has enough impulsion to start the half-pass [thanks to the use of the inside leg].

General rules: act sparingly during the movement. Take and give and don't block the horse.

When you lose control of the speed, it is because the horse is starting to be in charge.

Always precede the action of the hand with an adjustment of the torso. Otherwise we only concern ourselves with the horse's head. For example, to slow down the horse, get taller and arch the back a little [before using the hand].

With a young horse, when you go from sitting trot to posting trot, take a slightly lighter contact so the horse can lower his head a little.

To start the shoulder-in with a young horse in particular, do not use a strong action of the inside rein.

If you do not pass the corner properly (in walk or trot), you cannot have your horse properly straight on the long side.

If the shoulder-in is the continuation of the corner, it is easy; we will need much less aids.

In canter, see the horse can settle in his stride.

In the execution of an exercise, the intensity of the aid being used

---

progressively enlarged by both hands moving to the right and forward and some action of the left leg] must be adjusted as a function of the response of the horse to the demand.

Dressage training is the research of the purity of the walk, trot and canter.

At the conclusion of a clinic, Master Oliveira said: "Remember that it is the basic concepts that matter: the relaxation, the impulsion, the soft contact, the straight horse, the purity of the transitions, etc.."

Lesson to a group of riders on three and a half year old horses:
Principle: work in stages. The training of a young horse consists of passing from relaxation to a higher level of impulsion without getting excited.

So the *first objective* at the beginning of the lesson is relaxation in walk and trot.

Some advice: speak to the horse, caress, go back often to the lower neck position that stretches down, make sure that the horse enjoys himself in his movement ! Do some light shoulder-ins with a small angle started without force. Delicate gestures of the riders that don't surprise the horse, especially for the transition from walk to trot. Seek a relaxed trot.

During the trot, see if it is possible to increase the contact a little bit [making sure the horse is seeking the contact and the rider is not shortening the reins] and to obtain a little bit more vibration [energy].

Antoine riding Campo at the Hussière stables of Hélène Arianoff, October 1987.

175

Return to complete relaxation as a reward; use subtle aids both for up and down transitions. That is the way to develop the sensitivity of the horse [*la finesse*].

Return to walk [after the trot work] and ask for a little more vibration and angle in the shoulder-in than you did before.

Return to trot, [with the horse] more "bubbly" [like a glass of good champagne], but always with the same [self-imposed] limitation and the same preoccupation: never reach excitement. In the crescendo of the energy of the work, there is a measure worthy of respect: always return to relaxation as a reward.

For the transitions, don't surprise the horse but prepare by the quality of the exercise that precedes, and pass from one gait to the next without altering the state of mind of the horse.

For the transition from trot to canter, first obtain the correct trot with enough vibration so you don't need to use too strong a touch to obtain the canter.

Chapter 12

SAMPLES OF LESSONS AND EXERCISES
TO BE PRACTICED WITH YOUNG HORSES

After some transitions from walk, to trot, to canter, with the horse in good impulsion, return to the walk. Circle with shoulder-in. Then after the second corner [of the short side] change rein on the diagonal using the outside aids. Therefore, if the horse starts on the left rein use the right rein and right leg, so the horse performs a diagonal in a slight shoulder-in right. In addition, when on the diagonal lengthen the reins progressively so the horse reaches the wall with his nose on the ground. Then progressively take the reins back in the contact.

Note: be careful to always keep the same cadence, otherwise the exercise is without value. This exercise can be done at the trot also.

Sequence to perform with young horses:
1. Warm up for a few minutes in posting trot with long reins in a trot that is ample and active.
What Matters:
- good position of the rider,
- don't prod with the spurs,
- don't pull on the reins,
- control [the gaits] with the rider's torso.
2. Let the horse fall into the canter with the reins somewhat free.
Free canter, ample but not rushed (circles then go large [around the arena] then circles again).
3. Return to the walk. Do serpentines to organize the walk.
4. Then return to the trot, but a trot that is more regular, a little shorter, the reins a little more adjusted, in a position close to the *ramener*, but is not yet the *ramener* [the head not quite yet on the vertical].
5. Lengthen the trot, let the horse fall back into canter on circles.
6. Then let the horse return to the trot by abandoning the reins (circles, then going large, then changes of rein), then while the horse is trotting on the circle, push forward while fixating the fingers until the horse comes up on the hand and yields the poll.

Lesson with a rider on a four-year-old stallion.

First, warm-up work in relaxation and progressively push the horse forward while seeking the cadence. Then, transitions trot to walk to trot. In these transitions, prevent the horse from putting weight on his shoulders at the moment of the transition[196]. He must be flexible and light and not offer to resist.

If he gets over-bent by arching the neck too much, lift the hand on the snaffle and do some small vibrations on the snaffle from down to up on a rein that is slightly slack.

After a few transitions try to feel that the horse is sitting a little more and is rounder and see if the rider can feel the benefit of those transitions. Then go into shoulder-in at the walk.

Then trot on a circle and when the rider feels the horse is cadenced do shoulder-in on the same rein (the right rein when going to the right).

Then take the diagonal with the horse *still bent to the right but not in half-pass, this is a preparation to the half-pass.* It is necessary that this work happens without the horse running, in cadence, while paying attention to all the details.

Then perform transitions trot to canter to trot. "Before the transition from trot to canter, ask for a trot with more impulsion."

To finish: You can now start the halts and a few steps of reinback. Be very gradual.

Ophélie, a three and a half year-old filly ridden in the snaffle.

Note: This young filly has the peculiarity of not staying immobile in the halt. She moves and swings the croup.

The work explained below was performed on several days.

Samples of the work:

Walk slowly, think of the mental attitude of the horse and speak to her to keep her calm. If she doesn't position her head correctly, put her on *small circles* at the walk bent toward the inside, like in shoulder-in and using an opening rein while slightly lengthening the outside rein.

Only use inside rein and leg.

Change hand.

Do some halts from the walk at the place chosen by the rider, preferably along the wall immediately after the circle.

Halt with the minimum of aids ("by mere thought"), by lifting the hands without pulling backwards or by lifting only the inside hand, while the outside hand remains parallel to the inside one.

If needed, do a little vibration on that rein.

---

196   [by bringing the torso up and supporting the wrists]

Do not halt if the walk is not calm. Halt in a walk that contains the halt; do not halt if the horse is not in that particular walk.

Do not shorten the reins, otherwise she would lean on the reins, creating weight resistances and, by doing so, she would have a walk that is too fast[197].

Go into trot: a calm, medium trot on the circle[198].

Return to walk and perform a few more halts.

Then trot a little more active and during that trot, alternate yielding and re-taking the contact delicately, so the filly doesn't fall asleep on the contact [and start leaning].

Do a lot of patting.

Do a little bit of canter from the trot.

If the horse gets excited, return to walk and repeat the sequence.

Go to the trot only if she is calm in the walk, and go to the canter only if she is calm in the trot.

In the canter when we feel she is quiet, let go of the reins and take the contact again delicately, while talking to her.

Then let her fall back into the trot.

Go back to the canter (circle - go large [around the arena] - circle again).

Let her fall back into trot, then into walk, more by using the voice than the reins. The reins can be used later.

Advice: don't stay long on the same circle, [it is better] to change location in the arena frequently.

Ophélie the next day:

First, *free* walk on a long rein.

Then place the hands a little higher and slow down the walk progressively.

Then try a little shoulder-in on the long side [of the arena].

Then do the same work as the day before: halts and little circles in walk.

Then trot with variations of the gait: first a little slower then a little faster while respecting the principle: "hands without legs, legs without hands." Mix the posting trot with the sitting trot. Perform serpentines at the trot and go deep into the corners.

Then depart into canter. Alternate trot and canter while circling and going large [around the arena]. Push forward and pat the horse a lot

197   [The lightness of the contact is directly related to the balance and the cadence]

198   [This reference to medium trot only means a little more than an active working trot, not a true medium trot as performed in a dressage test.]

179

[for reassurance]. Use the inside rein to go from canter to trot.

This is when an incident occurred and the mare showed *disobedience:* while she was on a circle to the right rein the mare escaped suddenly by spooking to the left before returning to the wall.

What must be the response of the rider [in this situation]? He or she must have an instantaneous reflex that straightens the horse and brings her back to turning right and going forward by the *right rein "of domination."* This consists with the left rein loose, of lengthening the right rein [enough] and lowering it instantaneously, going - in the full domination rein - until bracing the right hand behind the knee and blocking it in the fold of the knee, while pushing the horse forward. The abruptness of the defense of the horse imposes an equally abrupt reaction from the rider. Victory is achieved by this condition. Yield when the horse yields.

After the domination of the horse, go back to working at the walk: circles and halts on the wall[199].

Advice to the lady rider: (the mare is on the left rein), if she wants to deviate her croup to the left at the moment of the halt, give a little tap of the whip on the left flank and start to frame her between the aids just a little bit.

The following day with Ophélie:
At the walk, some little circles while trying to get her to lengthen the neck and look down and toward the center of the circle[200] in cadence while feeling that the back is coming up.

Feel that the inside [of the mare] is relaxed. Act with the inside leg from back to front and feel that the side of the horse follows the movement of the leg.

Advice: If the filly falls a little bit toward the inside of the circle (to the left) put the left hand to the right and fix it (like a side rein) and act with the left leg.

At the trot: do the same circles as at the walk. Look for a release [to the hand]. Pay attention to the regularity of the cadence.

Practice numerous halts.

From the posting trot, do a few strides at the sitting trot (as a result the horse should reduce the stride and slow down the trot).

The mare must lengthen the trot when the rider goes back to the posting trot (in an energetic gait that is not rushed).

---

199   [When using the word domination, Nuno Oliveira is always referring to taking control of the situation by bring the horse back to the original movement]
200   [This must be done]

180

[Alternating between posting and sitting trot] is *how we begin* to teach the young horse to follow the influence of the torso and the seat and not only the arms and legs.

Depart into canter [from the trot]. Push the horse forward and, at the same time, caress the neck with one hand, then the other. Caress until she canters completely calmly. Let her fall back into the trot.

Ophélie six months later (May 1977), the mare has just turned four.

During this lesson, this is the exercise required: while at the walk on the left rein, take the center line, then perform a half-pass to the right [all the way to the wall], next do a right counter-shoulder-in [tracking left]. [Take the next diagonal] and change rein in right shoulder-in. Circle in right shoulder-in to the right. Turn on the center line again and half-pass to the right all the way to the wall, while paying attention [to the following]:

1. To the regularity of the walk,

2. That the horse doesn't resist on the inside rein (which is the right rein), [something] the mare has a tendency to do often,

3. Yield and re-take [the contact] often (particularly the inside rein).

Do more shoulder-ins both on the straight and on the circle while sometimes opening the inside rein followed by a release.

During another lesson

Same work as in the preceding lesson.

And on the circle: transitions walk-trot

Take and give as often as possible.

Perform shoulder-in left on the circle at the trot. Pay attention that the trot is not altered.

Vary the positions of the hand in order to feel [which position is most effective] at getting her light (practice trial and error all the time).

It is important to maintain the same speed.

Serpentine, counter-shoulder-in, circles.

Shoulder-in on the circle.

Shoulder-in down the long side.

Take the diagonal.

Perform counter-shoulder-in on the short side and shoulder-in on the diagonal.

Serpentine, while practicing the yielding of the hand each time the mare changes direction, without changing the speed.

Go into a more energetic trot: working trot posting. Choose the right moment to sit down in the collected trot when all the resistances have vanished.

"Maybe place the hands a little higher [with the reins] less taught and take and give (for mere fractions of seconds)."

"It is by respecting all the small details [of handling the horse] during the transitions that you prepare for collection."

Following lesson (during which Ophélie will create some difficulties at the trot on the right rein).

Work at the walk and trot.

Do a small circle, without resistance and without weight [on the reins], in the second corner [of the arena] before starting the shoulder-in on the long side.

Do another small circle just the same at the end of the shoulder-in.

If the mare resists: stop her by using a limited domination rein, [with an intensity] proportionate to the resistance.

It is necessary that the horse [reaches for the connection] on the inside rein and that the rider yields when the horse yields. At the trot to the right, we need to use this right opening rein [with the hand positioned away from the neck] to prevent the horse from running. It is the inside rein and leg that control the speed.

If the mare wants to run, or resists in particular with the inside rein that can be transformed--in the necessary measure--by a rein of domination (hand that becomes fixed and open toward the inside[201]).

Use vibrations if needed, then halt [the horse].

Therefore (Nuno Oliveira brings it back to our attention) the rider must use the inside leg and rein.

Rule: - Resist when she resists (resisting is never pulling[202]).

- Yield as soon as the mare yields.

Another technique to deal with this resistance to the right: on the circle to the right, do a few trot steps, halt, a few more trot steps, halt[203].

When she runs, enter into a small circle.

[Nuno Oliveira says to the rider:] "The more you let her run, the more she will become excited"[204].

---

201   [of the bend. Concrete hand as Nuno Oliveira mentioned several times before.]
202   [it is holding in place without moving the hand backwards]
203   [This is the principle of separation of force (resistance) and movement, an idea promoted by Baucher]
204   [One of the principles of training is to "prevent the evasion"]

182

The following lesson with Ophélie

This lesson was shorter because the one the day before was very long.

Nuno Oliveira advises the rider to caress as much as possible if the horse goes well.

However, if she resists, it is necessary to work until she yields.

"If you see that she has yielded to your last demand to the right, start to work on the left."

Advice: "In the case of *Ophélie* [who found the right bend more challenging], when you do ask for a bend to the right, your inside (right) leg must act more than your inside (left) leg when you do a bend to the left."

He also said: "When she yields, go large and caress immediately."

Lesson for a horse that has a neck that is too flexible.
"Turn like a stick"[205].

Place [in the *ramener*] your horse with the outside rein, don't let the head come toward the inside. Turn slightly sideways. This technique can advantageously replace the draw reins because it doesn't have their inconvenience (the risk of over-flexing the neck). It is a more delicate manner of positioning the horse. We work his haunches. It consists of turning the shoulders on a diagonal around the haunches. The horse must not bend left nor right, he must turn in one piece. Keep the hands fixed and turn by the seat, by your legs and by the angle of the reins [acting both together]. If he resists, halt, place the horse at the halt [place the forehead on the vertical] and start again.

Halt for the young horse.

For the young horse, the halt is an exercise that calms him and relaxes him. This is why at this stage of the work on mental and physical relaxation, it is useful to halt frequently first from the walk[206].

Before starting again, wait until he stays quiet for a few seconds, in peace. To halt is to put the horse in a state of calm and attention so he can start again immediately and remain calm.

Therefore we must push [the horse with the waist] for the halt.

We must not halt in any old fashion, but rather choose a place where the horse is straight, not only for the spectator, but also in the feeling [of symmetry that he gives to the rider].

205   [The idea is to do a turn that has no bend at all in which the spine stays completely straight in the turn]
206   [Halt by raising the hand and vibrating if needed, but not by pulling back]

After the halt, the horse must start again without falling on one shoulder or the other. At this stage we are not seeking the perfect straightness of the position (head and legs). He is not ready to halt with his neck positioned [in *ramener*]. We seek a quiet horse that is tranquil, relaxed in his brain, and is as straight as possible [for that stage of training], while creating in the halt the desire to step forward easily. We can use the voice aid to halt. Start again on a loose rein, because it is too soon to start on adjusted reins. After a halt it is the rider who must give the signal to start. Only give the signal if you feel the horse entirely quiet in his body. We can ask for the halt at the end of a circle. In that case, be sure to perform it in both directions.

It is a good idea to adjust the reins to a length that the horse halts by the action of the [rider's] torso and not by traction on the reins. *By this practice, we habituate the horse to responding to the action of the torso.* The reins adjusted to a certain length will certainly act, but as a result of the action of the torso. After some time, try to do the same thing from the trot. If the trot is too quick, slow it down (circles, serpentines, etc.). First, establish a regular trot before doing a circle. The halts aiming at relaxing the horse are done from the sitting trot, not the posting trot. After a halt from the trot on a circle, don't start into the trot, but rather into the walk before returning to the trot (at least at this stage of training). Those are halts that are neither square nor positioned in the neck, but halts to relax [the horse]. This is the first thing to do before positioning the head and neck. It is putting him in the state of mind suitable to make him accept the rest of the work. A young horse must be able to go into the corners, make round circles and halt without getting excited. The rest will follow. If we position his head too soon, he will revolt. It is after this stage and not before that we can start the dressage training of the horse.

Horse that sticks [leans on] *to the legs.*

For a horse which blocks the action of the leg[207], do not use the reins nor the spurs. Instead, give some taps with the whip just until he goes forward, for this will relax him without using force. Reduce the aids without abandoning the horse.

Rhythm: In every gait, when the horse has become pleasant to ride without the support of the aids and with a steady position, the horse will have achieved his tempo [*rythme*], his cadence. Do not confuse [a slow cadence] with laziness.

---

207   [refuses to go forward from the legs, which is common with young horses]

184